# Enslavers
## of
# the Maritimes

# Brenda J Thompson

Author of
A Wholesome Horror

Enslavers of the Maritimes
© 2024 Brenda J. Thompson

Cover design: Rebekah Wetmore, from an image by Tim Wilson
Editor: Andrew Wetmore

ISBN: 978-1-998149-26-1
First edition January, 2024

**MOOSE HOUSE**
PUBLICATIONS

2475 Perotte Road
Annapolis County, NS
B0S 1A0

moosehousepress.com
info@moosehousepress.com

We live and work in Mi'kma'ki, the ancestral and unceded territory of the Mi'kmaw people. This territory is covered by the "Treaties of Peace and Friendship" which Mi'kmaw and Wolastoqiyik (Maliseet) people first signed with the British Crown in 1725. The treaties did not deal with surrender of lands and resources but in fact recognized Mi'kmaq and Wolastoqiyik (Maliseet) title and established the rules for what was to be an ongoing relationship between nations. We are all Treaty people.

## Also by Brenda J. Thompson

Tales from the End of the Old Military Road (also from Moose House)

A Wholesome Horror: Poor Houses in Nova Scotia

Finding Fortune: Documenting and Imagining the Life of Rose Fortune

Single Mother's Survival Guide

# Endorsements

This book is a remarkably readable study of slavery in Colonial Canada. It takes a tremendous amount of information and presents it with impressive clarity. This book will be an essential contribution to the Canadian public's understanding of slavery.

Harvey Amani Whitfield,
Professor at the University of Calgary,
author of
*Biographical Dictionary of Enslaved Black People in the Maritimes*

Many books have been written about slavery in Canada, and in Nova Scotia in particular. Brenda Thompson calls slavery a terrible stain on our history which must not be repeated. Her Introduction is strong and powerful and is meant to ensure that this blight on our history is never forgotten. The extensive research that she has done for this book has brought back to life the names of many of those enslaved people and how some of them were treated. Never forget them.

This book is must have for all schools and libraries.

Sharon Robart-Johnson
author of *Two Sams*

Brenda J. Thompson's *Enslavers of the Maritimes* will strike some eyes as a shocking and most unwelcome revelation: that the ranks of colonial Nova Scotians, Islanders, and New Brunswickers included French, British, and Yankee slaveholders and slave-traders, all dead-serious about exploiting their human "property" and super-proud of their status.

Utilizing enterprising research into the lives of the enslaved Africans/Blacks, Thompson IDs the historic personages (pluto-crats, politicos, and oppressors) and illuminates their highfalutin belief that they could own another human soul.

Esteemed Maritime surnames like Wentworth, Haliburton, Salter, Inglis, Perkins, Hamilton, Campbell, and Savage are shown to have been the "handles" of enslavers. However, we also see that every escaping bondsperson (freedom-seeker) was engaged in a rite of exorcism: to rid themselves of the haunts who violated their integrity, those saltwater ghouls who ate up their substance and their surplus.

George Eliot Clarke
Author of *Whiteout: how Canada cancels Blackness*
Parliamentary Poet Laureate (2016-17)

# Foreword

I'm never going to be able to look at the Maritime landscape the same way ever again.

I live in Round Hill, in Nova Scotia's scenic Annapolis Valley. From my office window I can see glimpses of the meandering Annapolis River through the branches of an old maple. Our pre-Confederation home is located on a former apple farm, the remnants of which are still producing lovely fruit that is made into cider using a century–old wooden press.

My husband and I have a good life here. We say that, even when the weather is terrible, it's beautiful in the valley.

Yet, a few kilometers up the road there is another old property that overlooks the river. I have driven by it dozens of times, yet until Brenda Thompson handed me the manuscript to this book, little did I realize that the stately hillside house that presides over such a splendid, bucolic view was built by an enslaver.

Colonel James Delancey enslaved six people that we know of— Nance, Jane, Harriet, Charles, Jack and Caesar. And we might never even know of these folks if not for Jack's escape from his captor, which led to a famous "runaway slave" trial.

But let's talk about the "old major" first. According to an entry in a 1991 edition of *The Nova Scotia Genealogist*, Delancey led a "plantation lifestyle". While the entry does not indicate what that means, my imagination assumes something like a junior, northern version of southern plantations in the US, where black people worked the land and tended the house and family under duress, with every possible freedom either eclipsed or severely monitored —from thought and education to movement. Basic human rights. Basic humanity.

The entry, recorded in this book, describes how Delancey would have guests over for dinner and, in an act of narcissistic, macabre entertainment, would direct a young enslaved girl to stand still in the garden. She would be wearing a yellow turban. Delancey claimed he could shoot her turban right off her head, and then did.

"The turban would fall, and the girl would be unharmed."

'Unharmed' meaning not shot, remaining intact so she could

serve once again as a human prop in a parlour trick; an enslaved magician's assistant, if you will.

Life carried on until, in 1801, one of Delancey's slaves, Jack, ran away and made it to Halifax, where he found employment. When this was discovered, the enslaver sent a lawyer to Jack's employer demanding that his wages be turned over. An "act of trover" is a common law term in which there is an attempt to recover the value of chattels or goods wrongfully converted by another to his or her own use.

Delancey died before the case was resolved, failing at that point to regain possession of Jack. But the entire affair became one of the foundations for the abolition of slavery in Nova Scotia.

I cannot help but think of this every time I drive past that house now on my way to Bridgetown. And when I head the other way, toward Digby, as I circle around the hairpin turn at Clementsport and drive past a large, old building hugging the road. Built by Captain Douwe Ditmars, it was an inn where Eliza, her children Anthony and Eliza, and one other "unknown" were enslaved. Later, his son John would enslave someone named Dinah and six other "unknowns."

I drive around now looking at old properties with different eyes. You know that moment in the movie The Matrix when Neo can finally see that his surroundings are all code? Looking upon the idyllic landscape that is the Annapolis Valley is like that, having learned that goodly chunks of the settlers were enslavers. And I wonder: how many "unknowns" could have lived in those pretty, old homes?

Unknowns.

Unnamed, unrecorded. No faces. No family stories. No mourning in death. Unmarked graves. No legacies. They may have been old or young. Children. Babies.

Erasure is a theme that arises insidiously throughout Brenda's stark catalogue of enslavers.

While in the last couple of decades black scholars, writers and historians have sought to find those lost personalities and not only record but elevate them in print and film, there is an overall dearth of records of enslaved peoples in not only the Maritimes but in Canada in general. It comes as a surprise to many, including me, that slavery was an active institution in this country. The resounding myth is that Canada was the promised land to those who made it here through the Underground Railroad. While that is true, it is the preferred narrative over that of the enslaver and enslaved.

For example, in 2023 there was much fanfare not far from where I live about granting a house one of those historic plaques. The de Gannes-Cosby house in Annapolis Royal was built in 1708 over an Acadian cellar and is lauded as a rare example of pre-expulsion Acadian architecture.

Here's part of the description from the Government of Canada's website entry for National Historic Sites:

> The house was built in 1708 for Major Louis-Joseph de Gannes de Falaise, a French nobleman and officer with the garrison, who had arrived in Port-Royal in 1701. It was constructed on the foundations of an earlier house which had been razed during the 1707 siege of Port-Royal by the British. After the final capture of Port-Royal by the British in 1710, de Gannes de Falaise returned to France and the house was forfeited to the British Crown. It later served as the residence of the lieutenant-governor of the fort and town, beginning with Major Alexander Cosby. Cosby and, after his death in 1742, his wife Anne Winniett lived in the house from 1727 until 1788.

The de Gannes-Cosby House is located at 477 St. George Street, within the Annapolis Royal Historic District.

What is conveniently left out of the description on the website and on the plaque in front of the house is that Anne (Winniett) Cosby enslaved three people. Agatha, Rose and John Bulkely lived there. Surprise!

The same can be said for the Sinclair Inn Museum in Annapolis Royal. Owner Frederick Sinclair enslaved a person named Jane, yet there is nary a reference to her in the historical description of the building online or on site.

We don't know what happened to Jane, but we do know that when Anne Cosby died in 1788, the enslaved were "manumitted". An online search revealed that this practice has been in place since Roman times. It is viewed as a generous and compassionate act by an enslaver to allow a person or people freedom only after their captor is dead and doesn't need them anymore.

That theme of the benevolent owner pervades Canadian records. Slaves are referred to as "servants", lending enslavement a softer tone. Historians have dealt a kind hand to enslavers in this country, promoting the idea that there was a gentler sort of existence here, where families were closer to their enslaved folks and therefore more personally invested in them.

However, that intimacy is a two-edged sword.

The website for the Canadian Museum for Human Rights contains an article written by Steve McCullough and Matthew McRae about black slavery in Canada. They describe Canada as a "society with slaves" rather than a "slave society." They write:

At the time, much of the Caribbean and the southern United States were slave societies. There, large-scale slave labour on plantations was a dominant force in economics, politics and culture.

Enslaved people made up a smaller proportion of the population in early Canada than in plantation economies. This meant they toiled in relative isolation, which inhibited the creation of shared community. It possibly enabled even more intense surveillance by white society.

It might appear contradictory, but after reading this text, the theme of erasure is treacherously tied to the theme of surveillance. It appears that no one cared about the lives of enslaved persons until they weren't there—either the enslavers (as in by death) or the enslaved. If someone escaped captivity, then suddenly they were described in minute detail—their gender, stature, what they wore, what they "stole".

I imagine it being much like taking stock after a house fire or a theft—you don't talk about what you lost until it's gone. That heirloom teapot, jewelry, your pets...except these records and conversations aren't about stuff. They are about humans. It's not like someone broke into your shed and took the snowblower. A person decided to claim their own agency and left.

And enslavers took great umbrage at this haughty action. Like Colonel Delancey, they would put ads in newspapers looking for help in recovering their supposed property.

Sometimes they'd get them back. Sometimes not. And I wonder if it was even about the money.

Reading some of the entries in this text, I can see evidence of rampant narcissism. To have a slave decide they don't want to be one anymore seems like some kind of personal affront. How dare they! Perhaps it is because land properties were not as vast as the deep-South plantations that a more intimate relationship between enslavers and their captives was inevitable.

There are some chilling descriptions in this book that reveal the level to which enslaved persons were not only gazed upon but studied and behaviourally judged.

For example, George Cornwall of Granville Township enslaved three "unknowns" and, upon his death, directed in his will that his wife "manumit and set free by her will after decease, but in case they do not behave as honest or orderly servants, I wish that she should sell them as undeserving of her or my intended bounty towards them" (my italics). Cornwall's overt need for control of his slaves' behaviour extended beyond death.

In another entry an enslaver sells off a woman for having a child out of wedlock. John Seigneur, a Louisbourg innkeeper, had purchased 25 year old Louise from a Quebec slaver, but upon her arrival found that she was heavily pregnant, possibly from having been raped on board the ship delivering her. Seigneur was furious because his purchase "gave a poor example to his family, especially his young daughters", not to mention that she couldn't work as hard. Louise delivered her child but four months later she and her baby were sold in Martinique. She was replaced by a 14 year old boy named Etienne.

This description of behavioural surveillance left my blood running cold. Susan Barclay was married to Major Thomas Barclay of Annapolis Royal (an MLA) who enslaved two "unknowns". The entry is chilling:

> Mrs. Barclay was said to have been cruel to her slaves. These stories are likely exaggerated, yet there must have been some foundation for them. [Again, the attempt at softening the severity of an enslaver's actions.] There have been accounts of slaves tied by their thumbs in the attic, of a slave girl stealing pie and being made to crawl into the hog pen, retrieve and eat the crusts she had thrown there. The most horrifying story concerns a slave murdered and sealed up in a fireplace, and this last is supposed to account for the ghost claimed to be that of Mrs. Barclay.

Even in gruesome death a slave is nameless, their afterlife being absorbed/appropriated by their enslaver.

Colonel Henry Denson of Falmouth was a non-Planter settler who brought with him at least a dozen enslaved people from the United States. He was apparently so strict, "he asked his slaves to bury him in an upright position when he died so he could continue to watch over them."

They didn't. After noticing Denson's forehead breaking into a sweat three days after his supposed death, they buried him ten feet down and piled rocks on his grave. Just to be sure.

Again, what kind of person is so authoritarian and narcissistic as to think they can control the lives of others beyond death? And expect his captives to actually obey his command?

These are just some examples of the many names, places, and stories recorded in this book. I find myself keeping the manuscript handy so when I come across a historical family name, I can quickly look it up to see if there is an enslaver legacy attached to it. Indeed, I did a check to find out whether my own property was part of that hideous institution (it's not, phew).

So, what if someone finds that their family's ancestor is recorded? What will their reaction be? Anger? Shame? Denial? Dismissal? Acknowledgment? Atonement? I am curious. As the first-born Canadian of immigrants, I don't have this legacy. Directly, that is. My ancestry is English, which means my heritage is indubitably tied with the economic advantages of enslavement, then and now. Regardless of whether my family's name is in here, I am living in an area where enslavers settled. I have to own that. I enjoy the legacy of those unnamed folks who toiled here without freedom of movement or any sort of bodily agency. It behooves me to remember them. And it makes me wonder how to go forward with this knowledge.

The contents within appear spartan and but are far from antiseptic. While this is a likely incomplete cataloguing of settler behaviour, attitudes, activities, and overt racism, it provides a minute insight into what occurred right here in our midst. I am forever changed by this information.

That it is presented by a white settler is appropriate. The author is to be lauded for handling the information as an objective collection of research without the overtones of a white saviour mentality. Mind you, having this information revealed by a white person may realistically hasten the possibility of the contents herein becoming more widespread rather than having them cornered as a minority-group interest.

Indeed, I am curious to see what the impact of this book will be on recorded history in general. Will there be names added to historic plaques? Will unmarked graves be sought out? Will there be archaeological digs commissioned? How will we, as a white collective, respond to this knowledge? What will it mean for the Black and Indigenous communities of the Maritimes to have this acknowledgement?

There are stories here that have forever burned their way into my existence. Colonel Delancey's callous treatment of that poor girl in the yellow turban, the one who had to stand there while he shot at her, is just one of them. Oh, by the way, at some point she took the opportunity to add some arsenic to his coffee and killed him.

Linda Hulme Leahy,<br>
Freelance writer and editor<br>
January, 2024

# Introduction

This will not be an easy book to read. Those of us who have compassion for other human beings will have to read it slowly, and process bit by bit the cruelty that Maritimers did to other Maritimers simply because of the pigment colour in their skin and because they had a different culture to that of European descendants. Kidnapping, murder, rape, child molestation, and confinement all took place, and yet we do not know much about this history.

Why?

History is not always stories of pride and patriotism. History will often upset you if you dig deeper than the superficial education provided in public schools. Much of our history is based on genocide, violence, and blood. Much of our history happens because of 'leaders' whose ideas are based on themselves and a small group of (usually) men getting more power and money than those of us who are less interested in power, money and privilege.

Ordinary people are often forced into battles, wars, and performing duties that we would really rather not participate in. Mental/physical coercion and 'brainwashing' take place, and there we are, doing things we would not normally do, to keep the peace in our own communities and for 'the sake of the nation'. History is written to glorify the 'winners'; those with wealth, power and privilege.

If they do discuss enslavement, our history books have 'whitewashed' the history. Remember the Heritage Moment commercial put out by the Canadian Government several years ago in which a married African American enslaved couple are reunited after being smuggled out of the southern United States into Canada? It was warm and fuzzy and totally whitewashed. It gave the impression that Canada was a beacon of hope for African slaves if they could only make it to Canada. This was true for 31 years.

But this commercial failed to mention that, for the preceding 205 years in what became known as the country of Canada, enslavement of Africans happened. How tidy and convenient of us to forget that history.

Researchers and writers of Enslaved African people of the Maritimes, Whitfield and Cahill, called it a 'historic amnesia'[1]. Masters' Degree student Sarah Elizabeth Chute, refers in her thesis to the history of enslavement in Canada as "historiographic lacuna"[2].

But what we call 'amnesia' or 'forgetting' is actually nothing of the sort. We know slavery in Canada happened, but we deliberately choose not to remember. We choose not to research it, write about it, read about it, teach it, or discuss it, so we are not forgetting, we are wilfully choosing not to remember.

If someone does remember and bring up slavery during a class or conversation, or in a political setting, we revise our history by referring to ourselves as white people in Canada as being 'nice' to our slaves. It was slavery. There is absolutely nothing 'nice', redeemable, generous or positive about slavery or enslavement.

Let's look at how we wrote about enslavement in the past. In my own area of Annapolis Royal Nova Scotia, F. W. Harris wrote in a paper he presented at the Annual Meeting of the Historical Association of Annapolis Royal on November 11, 1920:

> Generally speaking the treatment given to this class of servants by their different masters while living in the county was of a generous nature, and we have many instances recorded by means of last wills and testament where proprietors of these negro servants in bondage were not unmindful of their servitude to them, and in the number of ways showed their appreciation.[3]

Notice the use of the word 'servant' in this quote. What an insulting word used to cover up what was really happening; slavery.

In 1713 a French priest brought his enslaved boy to Louisbourg with him when he relocated from Quebec to the Cape Breton fortress. He referred to the boy as his 'slave'. By the time the British Americans arrived in Nova Scotia seventy years later, they were calling their enslaved people, 'servants'.

As the Ku Klux Klan used hoods to hide their identities from

---

1 Whitfield/Cahill *Slave Life and Slave Law*, p.31

2 Chute, *Bound to Slavery*, p. 5

3 Harris, F.W. "Negro Population" p. 4

what they were (and are) doing, the British used the word 'servant' to hide what they were doing. Both groups used concealment because they knew what they were (and are) doing was wrong on several different levels. The British used the word 'servant' to hide what they were actually practising, which was slavery. This use of language helped them quell their collective consciousness and guilt while continuing to enslave human beings.

For 150 years, many other researchers, historians and biographers of Enslavers continued to perpetuate this language of invisibility of enslavement by omitting the fact that the Enslaver abused other human beings. They continued to use the word 'servant', thus ensuring 'politeness' of enslavement because white people felt uncomfortable about this part of our history.

The term 'pedagogy of discomfort' is often used while reading academic articles about slavery in the Maritimes. The discomfort is the feelings of white people who are reading about it. Imagine being an African Maritimer whose ancestors were enslaved and reading about 'discomfort'. How enraging!

I did not write this book to shame anyone's ancestors, but rather to specify the white side of Maritime Black History that we don't like to talk about. By not identifying and recording the ancestors who enslaved other human beings, we are literally 'whitewashing' our history.

But how can we forget or ignore the story of thousands of people in the Maritimes who were raped, imprisoned, kidnapped, murdered, and brutalized by thousands of other Maritimers?

When you mention slavery in the Maritimes, the people who do know about it often dismiss the atrocities committed by the Enslavers by stating that it was 'in the past', that we should 'let it be' and 'I wasn't there. I wasn't alive then, so I am not responsible.'

We estrange ourselves from our history by refusing to recognize the severity and horror of what was done. When we estrange ourselves from our history, we have more of a chance of repeating it. And this was a very unflattering part of our history that we should never repeat.

We are also refusing to recognize how much our families, our communities, and our provinces have benefited from enslavement. In my own Annapolis County, where there was a fair amount of slavery, I drive down the road and see centuries-old homesteads and 200+ year-old houses where I know enslaved people were forcibly kept and made to labour. I think of how much the enslavement built up the wealth of that family, that farm, that community.

Yet none of it is recognized. Instead we recognize and revere the name of the Enslaver. How is that ethical? How is that justice for the enslaved?

To know our history helps us not only be aware of our past (with all its glories and sins) but also shape our future. We build our future from the cold, stark realities of our past rather than deluding ourselves that our ancestors did not do the things they did, such as enslave other human beings.

When the Loyalists arrived, with their enslaved 'servants', they brought another 'problem' with them. During the War of Independence in the United States, the British offered freedom to any enslaved African who ran away from their 'Master' and joined the British side to fight against the rebels. Many Africans took advantage of that offer, employing their own resources to run away from their 'Masters' and get to a British ship, camp or city. Many ran to Augustine, Florida where they were then brought to the Maritimes as 'Free Negroes'.

The problem became differentiating an Enslaved Negro from a Free Negro. How to tell the difference? Some Maritimers did not care whether a Black person was 'free' or not and re-enslaved people such as Mary Postill and her daughters. Chute wrote in her thesis:

> The region, then, existed as a site of freedom while it simultaneously functioned as a site of enslavement. Although the legal differences between slavery and freedom were real, Black people in the Maritimes experienced racism and inequality regardless of their status...Through exploitation, indentured servitude, and slavery, many Black people in the Maritimes were unfree.[4]

The 'free negroes' often set up their own communities throughout the Maritimes, often referred to and named Birchtown after General Samuel Birch, who signed their Certificates of Freedom to live in the Maritimes.

It became known amongst the Enslavers that if their enslaved people could get to one of these Birchtown communities, they

---

4 Chute, p. 17

would be protected. Hence, many Enslavers considered Birch-towns to be a threat to their livelihood.

Meanwhile, some white Loyalists were doing critical thinking about their own fight for independence from Britain while enslaving Black people, and the contradiction that was presenting to their consciousness. This resulted in some white people either manumitting (freeing) their slaves and/or actively working in the abolition movement.

We often picture 'slavery' as what we have seen in books, documentaries and movies as taking place in the southern United States, with large plantations where the Africans lived in shacks and sheds, away from the Big House where their 'Masters' lived. This was not the reality in the Maritimes, however.

Dr. Harvey Amani Whitfield (University of Calgary) often refers to 'family enslavement', in which the enslaved person lived in the house with the family, ate meals with them and slept under the same roof. Sounds cosy, does it not?

But what if the family was abusive to you? What if they made you eat in a corner of the room rather than at the family table? What if you had no bed of your own but were expected to sleep by the hearth to keep the fire going all night? What if you, the enslaved, hated and despised the family you were enslaved to, but were forced to live with them with no break from your abuser?

As Harvey Amani Whitfield has more recently reminded us, 'family slavery' and the intimacy of master-slave relations in the North meant enslaved people suffered from the burden of proximity to their demanding Enslavers. Enslaved people in northern North America were vulnerable to acts of physical and sexual violence since their labour in households and on farms offered little distance from their Enslavers.[5]

Not so cosy after all.

For an enslaved female, it did not matter if you lived in the house or in a hut outside of the house; you were still considered to be sexually available to your 'Master', with no repercussions for rape and abuse. As an African Maritime female slave, you were also vulnerable to rape and sexual assault from enslaved men. Many of these enslaved men were swimming in (justifiable) rage and, seeking to relieve their anger, some turned to violence and abuse of those whom they felt were weaker than them: women and chil-

_____
5 Chute, p. 19

dren.

More recent writers tend to make light of enslavement in the Maritimes. Chute notes other researchers and writers of American and Canadian slavery:

> [Thomas Watson] Smith helpfully situates Maritime slavery within a continental framework through comparisons to the American states, but he oversimplifies the small-scale and often domestic nature of slavery in the Northern regions, including New England and the Maritimes, by describing it as 'mild'. [6]

Chute also quotes author Robin Winks' work on enslavement in Canada and their thoughts on how enslavers treated their slaves:

> ...far more positive evidence of humane treatment..' of enslaved people in Canada, citing instances of enslavers offering gifts, medical treatment, protection, and sometimes freedom.[7]

Lydia Jackson of Hantsport, Nova Scotia; Jupiter Wise of Charlottetown, Prince Edward Island; and Nancy of New Brunswick might disagree with this assumption of 'humane treatment'. Slavery in Canada was not "humane". It was enslavement. It was bad. It is a terrible stain on our history and we must never repeat it. Ever.

And that means we must never forget what happened, what we (our culture as European descendants) did and how our communities benefited from it.

Roland H. Sherwood wrote in his book *Pictou Pioneers* of a young man who ran away but was captured by his Truro enslaver:

> This man had a negro slave who ran away on several occasions, due to the harsh treatment he received. The only place other than Truro, that this slave knew, was Pictou. Once, when he had slipped away, he took the poor excuse of a road between Truro and Pictou. On the lone trail through the dense woods, the slave was easily overtaken. The irate owner at once proceeded to punch a hole in the lower ear

---

6 Chute p.19
7 *Ibid*, p. 21-22

lobe of the slave, through which he inserted the lash of his whip. Then mounting his horse he rode off toward Truro with the slave running behind at the end of the tether. [8]

We see many examples of manumission (another nice word that covers up many ills and sins) in wills of Enslavers in the Maritimes. The enslaved person was freed only *after* the Enslaver passed away. They still wanted the free labour of the person they enslaved until the day they died.

To force someone to serve you, to give up any semblance of their own life, their own decisions, and their own autonomy, until the day you die is not kindness; it is narcissistic exploitation of the person you are forcing to remain with and labour for your family.

When I was researching for this book, I wanted to look at the relationship between the Enslaver and the Enslaved. The manumissions of the Enslaved by the Enslavers through probate/wills often describe the enslaved in affectionate terms; others described the enslaved as though they were cattle and, indeed, lump them in with the cattle in their wills. Still others, concerned about how their family will get by without the forced labour of the enslaved if they were to run away, offered them land, money and other bribes to stay with the family after the 'Owner' has passed away.

The ads about runaway slaves, now called Freedom Seekers rather than Runaways, tell us that the Enslaver wanted his or her slave back because of money invested in the Enslaved, because the Enslaver wanted to punish them, because the Enslaver had a fondness for the Enslaved, or all of the above.

The Enslaved, however, were attempting to take control of their own lives by running away. They were Freedom Seekers. They did not like how they were being treated, they did not like where they lived or they simply did not want to be enslaved. And who would?? So they ran. Many of them successfully, as the advertisements indicate.

Do not make the assumption that only white men held slaves; white women were also active participants in enslavement. You will find a number of names of women who either inherited their slaves, were given them as a 'gift', or bought the slaves themselves.

The Widow Desmaret of Cape Breton owned three Enslaved people in 1739; Phebe, Mary and Jane Totten of Annapolis County,

---

8 Sherwood, Ronald H. *Pictou Pioneers*

Nova Scotia all shared a young Enslaved girl named Clarinda in 1788 and Margaret Murray of Halifax enslaved two women and one child in 1787. Sarah Cory of New Brunswick and Harriett and Louisa Haszhard of Prince Edward Island also enslaved other human beings.

The actions of the Freedom Seekers are invaluable in that they resulted in newspaper alerts and advertisements which tell us about a person who would be invisible if it were not for the advertisements. The ad can tell us what the enslaved person looked like, any distinguishing marks, voice accents, what they were wearing, how long they had been gone, and that they were courageous and resourceful enough to take the opportunity to run.

However, the ads also helped to perpetuate enslavement by publishing these advertisements to the public and asking the public to watch for the Freedom Seekers and report to authorities if they spotted a runaway.

These advertisements also tell us something about the Enslaver. They tell us how the Enslaver treated his or her slave. You will notice that some of the Enslavers put out multiple advertisements over several years regarding several enslaved runaways. The ads also tell us, by the tone of the language used, where the Enslaver thinks his slave is going to run to, how they are going to run away (usually ships are mentioned, this being the Maritimes), and how much money the Enslaver was willing to offer to get his Freedom Seeker back.

There are no recorded advertisements placed by women; all the ads were placed by men.

Chute writes of these ads in the abstract of her paper *Runaway Slave Advertisements from Loyalist Newspapers of the Maritime Colonies*:

> These advertisements reveal the presence of slavery Maritime colonies and explain the nature of slavery there. Comparisons between these advertisements and those from other British North American colonies complicate the traditional understanding of Canada as a land of freedom for many black people. Significantly, these advertisements also bear witness to the acts of resistance of courageous individuals who resisted the notion of bondage.[9]

---

9 Chute, S. E. *Abstract of Runaway Slave Advertisements*

The practice of enslavement of other human beings in the Maritimes ended in 1834 under British colonial law. It has been noted by some historians that most of the practice had ended well before that (early 1800s) because of the constant enslaved runaways who were finding freedom and protection in the Free Negro Communities in the province and by the legal cases in the colonial court system by the enslaved who challenged their enslavement.

As New Brunswick and Nova Scotia did not have a 'Slave Legislation' written in their books (Prince Edward Island was the only one of the Maritime Provinces to have legislation about enslaving people), the figurative door was opened for the enslaved and their allies to question whether slavery was legal in these two provinces. This was the argument used by lawyer Richard John Uniacke Jr. (whose wife, ironically, was an Enslaver) in the very important Delancey vs. Woodin case in Halifax.

Some of the Enslavers had to be forced to give up the humans they enslaved. One family, in particular in the Annapolis Valley is noted for being forced to set the Enslaved free.

It must be recorded, however, that the vast majority of Enslavers, when forced to let the Enslaved go free, did so by letting them have nothing more than the clothing they wore. They were put out to their 'freedom' with no land, no money, no resources, in a cultural system permeated with racism, to fend for themselves. All the work, the labour, the Enslaved had performed for the Enslaver was forgotten about as the formerly enslaved were put on the roads and the provincial governments and Britain made no resources available to help the suddenly-penniless, homeless, hungry people.

As a result, many of the formerly Enslaved ended up "indenturing" themselves to white men and women in order to survive. Many others put themselves up for auction in the annual parish poor auction, in which they offered their labour to the successful bidder for a year, so long as they were given food and shelter.

If you do a search of poor house records in areas that practised slavery, you will see the entrance of Black Molly, Black Jim or others who are described by using the word Black in front of their name or simply a single name with no surname.

They still were not free to have an autonomous life even after they gained their 'freedom'.

All of this is history we have rarely looked at, or looked at only if we are interested in the subject.

As we have learned the history of the Acadians and the *Grand Dérangement*, our hideous treatment of them, so should we learn the history of the Enslaved and the Enslavers in the Maritimes. It would be irresponsible of us to not know this. We need to discuss this stain on our history to ensure it never happens here again.

We shall all be ancestors to someone someday. Remember this.

BJT
Summer, 2023

**Dedicated to**

the people who suffered under enslavement,
who survived enslavement
and their descendants, who are
still dealing with the repercussions of enslavement.

This material is the product of extensive research and consultation with experts in the field. Any errors or omissions are the author's.

# Enslavers of the Maritimes

# Table of Figures

**Brenda J. Thompson**

# Enslavers of Nova Scotia

## Formerly known as Acadie
## Also known as L'nu

## A

Acker, Samuel
Chedabucto, Cumberland County, 1784
Enslaved one male known as Jack.
Loyalist
*Whitfield "Biographical" p. 99*

Ackerman, Johannes
Shelburne, Shelburne County, 1783
Enslaved three people, including at least two men: Sam and Harry.
*Whitfield "Biographical" p. 91*

Allardice, Archibald
Bookseller/ Naval Lieut. (ret)
Pictou County, 1784-86
Enslaved one male, Sambo (age 25).
Allardice bought Sambo from Dr. John Harris of Truro.
See *Harris, John* for a partial transcript of the Bill of Sale of Sambo.
*Whitfield "Biographical" p. 166*
*NSA Pictou County Reg.Deeds Vol1A P.223*

Allen, Ebenezer
Halifax, 1784
Enslaved one male, Isaac.
*Whitfield, "Biographical" p. 90*

Allen, Isaac (Lieut. Col.)
Wilmot, 1784
Enslaved seven people; all names unknown.
*Smith p. 24*

Alexander, James
Port Roseway, 1783
Enslaved two people: Sue (age 25), Charles (23).
*Whitfield, p. 176*
*Book of Negroes*
*Hodges Book No. 2, p. 145*

Allison, Joseph & Alice
Horton, 1807
Enslaved one female, Nelly (age 25).
In the Last Will & Testament, Joseph bought Nelly from his friend Simon Fitch and intends to leave Nelly to his wife along with an interesting insight:

> "...Have Granted, Bargained, and Sold and made over unto the said Simon Fitch a certain Negro woman named Nelly, of the age of twenty-five or thereabout, now in the possession of the said Simon, where she hath been since the said Second day of March last, which Negro woman was and is a part of the Personal Estate of the said Joseph Allison (if a Negro can be considered personal property in Nova Scotia)..."

*Whitfield, "Biographical", p. 138*
*Smith, p. 65-66*

Amberman, Mrs.
Granville Township, Annapolis County, 1797
Enslaved one female, Jane Japean (who married Caesar Hawkins of
Clementsport).
*March 11, 1797, Granville Township Book*

*Figure 1: The Amberman House in Granville Ferry, NS*

The Amberman estate is now known as The North Hills Museum. Think of Jane Japean when you visit the museum.

*NS Archives 1981-541 no. 446*

Andrews, Samuel
Shelburne Township, Shelburne County; moved to Yarmouth
County, 1786
Enslaved James Singletery, his wife and a child.
*Whitfield, "The Struggle over Slavery", p.33.*

*See next page.*

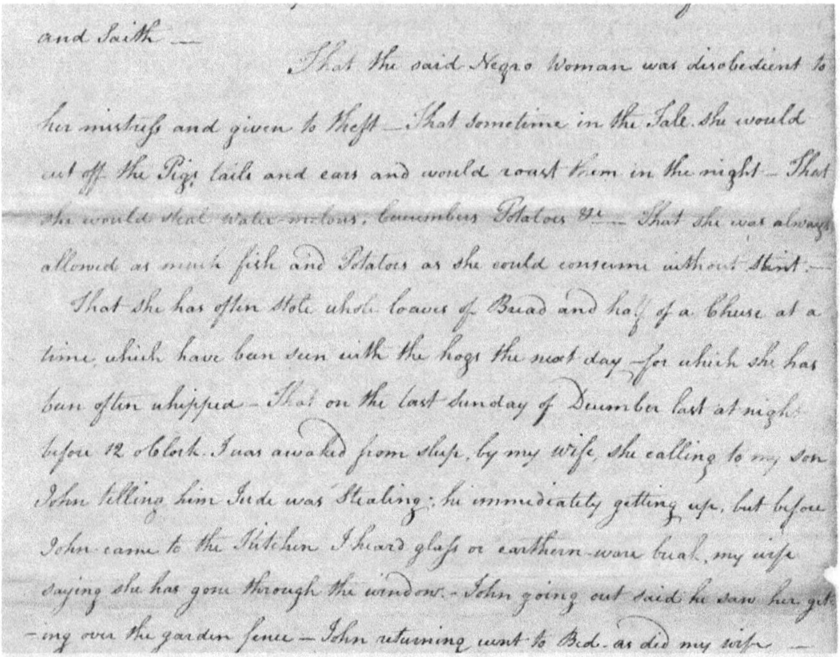
and Saith —
That the said Negro Woman was disobedient to her mistress and given to theft — That sometime in the Fall she would cut off the Pigs tails and ears and would roast them in the night — That she would steal Water-melons, Cucumbers Potatoes &c — That she was always allowed as much fish and Potatoes as she could consume without Stint. — That she has often stole whole loaves of Bread and half of a Cheese at a time, which have been seen with the hogs the next day — for which she has been often whipped — That on the last Sunday of December last at night before 12 oClock I was awaked from sleep, by my wife, she calling to my son John telling him Jude was Stealing; he immediately getting up, but before John came to the Kitchen I heard glass or earthern-ware break, my wife saying she has gone through the window. — John going out said he saw her get-ing over the garden fence — John returning went to Bed. as did my wife —

*Figure 2: From the transcript of the Andrews murder trial*
*NS Archives RG42 Shelburne Volume 1 File 43*

"Loyalist Samuel Andrews of Tusket River, Yarmouth County, and his sons Samuel and John were tried in 1801 for the murder of 'Jude', an enslaved woman, the previous year. The men claimed that her death was accidental. Medical evidence showed that she had been killed by a blow from a 'blunt pointed instrument.' A fellow enslaved woman, 'Diana', who referred to Jude as 'my sister', testified to having seen John and Samuel Andrews standing beside Jude, each with 'a stick about the size of an iron candle stick and of the length of my arm'. The jury acquitted Andrews. Samuel's wife Mary was also indicted but not tried."

*Shelburne County Special Court of Oyer and Terminer*
*Nova Scotia Archives RG 42 SH volume 1 file 4*

"In 1785 James Singletory "applied to James McEwen Esq [according to Benjamin Marston, McEwen was a justice of the peace], praying he might be discharged from the service" of Samuel Andrews. Andrews had migrated to Shelburne from Saint Augustine and claimed James 'as his slave.' He produced a pass signed by the commissary of claims of Charleston that Andrews had paid £50 for James, his wife and child. However, he did not produce a bill of sale....The court decided that Andrews had to produce 'due attested proof' before the court would send the family back into slavery. However, Andrews was allowed 'Twelve months' to obtain proof of ownership. James, his wife, and child were required to live with Andrews as servants throughout the 12-month period, while their owner attempted to find - or more likely to forge - a bill of sale....The court returned James to Andrews' service, even though he (James) had successfully challenged his bondage, and Andrews continued to own slaves through the 18th century."

*Whitfield, "The Struggle", p. 32*

*Figure 3: Painting of Shelburne with the barracks opposite, 1789*
*Government of Canada Historical Search recherche-collection-search.bac-lac.gc.ca/eng/Home/Search?q=shelburne %20ns&DataSource=Images*

Yarmouth County author Sharon Robart Johnson wrote *Jude and Diana*, an award-winning book about the murder of Jude. The Andrews brothers, accused of the murder of Jude, were acquitted. Most of the jury members were Enslavers.

Andrews, Robert
Port Roseway, 1783
Enslaved one male, Vulcan (age 18).
*Hodges, Book Two, p. 147*

Andrews, William
Windsor Township, 1794
Unsure if this man, Matthew Tucker, was enslaved by Andrews. The 1794 Census states that Tucker was 'living' with Andrews.
*States, p. 46*

Anderson, John
Lunenburg County, 1783
Enslaved two males: Harry (age 23) and William.
*Whitfield pp. 81, 232*

Allardice, Archibald
Pictou, 1786
Enslaved one man, Sambo (age 25), whom he sold to Dr. John Harris, also of Pictou.
*See Bill of Sale under Harris, John (Dr.)*
*Nova Scotia Archives, Pictou County Register of Deeds Vol. 1A p. 223 (microfilm 18475)*

Archibald, Matthew
Truro, 1779
Enslaved one person, Abram (age 12), whom he purchased from Matthew Harris of Pictou.
*See Bill of Sale under Harrison.*
*Nova Scotia Archives Colchester County Register of Deeds Vol. 1, p.*

*468 (microfilm 17438)*

Army & Navy (Department of)
1784, Chedabucto
Enslaved 'many', including Caesar, Jeffy, Plenty Platt, Harry Savage, Samuel Smith, Charles Swinney, George Young, York.
*Whitfield, Biographical, pp. 36, 102, 146, 174, 179, 228, 236*

Atkinson, Theodore
Louisbourg, Cape Breton, 1745
Enslaved one male, John Gloster.
*Donovan, Slaves and their Owners, p. 23*

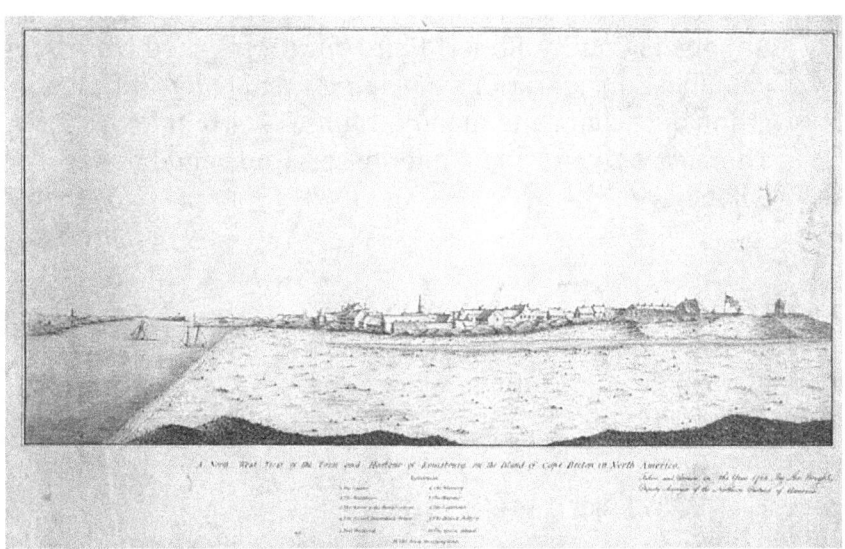

*Figure 4: The Fortress of Louisbourg, 1766*
*From Government of Canada Historical Collections*

Augruax, Pierre
Île Royale (Cape Breton), 1751
Enslaved one female whom he freed upon his death, Moll.
*Donovan, Slaves and their Owners, p. 23*

# B

Bacon, Daniel
Louisbourg, Cape Breton, 1745
Enslaved one male, Rueben.
*Donovan, Nominal, p. 157*

Baird, Robert
Bridgetown, 1779
Enslaved one male, Thomas, whom he manumitted.

> "Through an earlier instrument, drawn up in May, 1779, and recorded in the registry of deeds' office, Bridgetown, Annapolis County, Robert Baird 'for divers good Causes and Valuable Considerations me hereunto moving' did 'give, grant, quit-claim and manumitt unto a certain Negro named Thomas of all and all manner of servitude and bondage whatsoever...'"
>
> *Smith, p. 61*

Banks, (Ensign)
Clements Township , 1783
Enslaved on male child, John January (age 7).
*Whitfield, p. 100*
*Book of Negroes*

Bannier, Julien
Île Royale, 1742
Enslaved one male, Arny.

> "Arny, a Guadeloupe mulatto, likewise became a resident of the island, when Captain Pierre Cosset sold him to Julien Bannier for 800 livres."
>
> *Donovan, Slaves & their Owners p. 8*

Barclay, Andrew
Shelburne, 1783
Enslaved between five and seven people. Only known name is that of William.
*Whitfield, p. 211*

> Frost & States record Andrew Barclay as arriving in Shelburne with five servants with four children amongst them, in Section 3 of *King's Scholarly Inquiry...*, and that Andrew Barclay attempted to gain more land by hiring his own surveyor and claiming land that was set aside for Birchtown, the community of Free Blacks.
>
> Stephen Kimber also writes about this incident (pp.146-7) in his book about the founding of Shelburne, *Loyalists and Layabouts.*
>
> Barclay eventually settled for 200 acres on the east side of the Jordan River, calling it Barclay Valley.

Barclay, Thomas (Major) and wife Susan
Related to Andrew Barclay
Thomas and Susan started in Shelburne but then moved to Annapolis Royal in the 1780s.
Enslaved at least one male and one female.
MLA for Annapolis County in 1785.
*Perkins, p. 31*

> "Mrs. Barclay was said to have been cruel to her slaves. These stories are likely exaggerated, yet there must have been some foundation for them. Some slave owners are reputed to have thought severe punishment necessary. There have been accounts of slaves tied by their thumbs in the attic, of a slave girl stealing pie and being made to crawl into the hog pen, retrieve and eat the crusts she had thrown there. The most horrifying story concerns a slave murdered

and sealed up in a fireplace, and this last is supposed to account for the ghost claimed to be that of Mrs. Barclay."

*Perkins, p. 60*

Perkins may have believed that Susan Barclay's cruelty was exaggerated, but Smith records her cruelty, writing:

"Mrs. J.M. Owen, of Annapolis, to whom the writer of this paper has to express his indebtedness for more than one item of interest, has referred in the Halifax Herald to the tradition that Mrs. Barclay, wife of Colonel Barclay, of Annapolis, was responsible for the death of a slave through a severe whipping she had ordered of him."

*Smith, p. 77*

Barclay, Thomas and Wife
Shelburne, 1783-1791
Enslaved seven persons, including one female, Mertilla Dixon.
*Complaint of Mertilla Dixon, RG 34-321 M97 file NS Archives*
*Whitfield, p.211*

Barron, Edward (Captain)
Cumberland County, 1800
Enslaved one female, Phoebe, and one male child, Hugh, her son
*Whitfield, Biographical, p. 145*

"In his last will and testament, Barron made provisions for the freedom of Phoebe and her son Hugh, writing '...worldly estate which it hath pleased God to bless me with', Phoebe, his slave, was to have her freedom at his death, and her son, Hugh Cumming, at the age of twenty-one or sooner if she should wish. 'Let her have two cows and six ewes.'"

*Smith, p. 84*

Barronsfield, Cumberland County, was named after Edward Barron.

Barton, Joseph (Colonel)
Digby County, 1788
Enslaved one female, Hannah and her two children, William and another whose name we do not know, possibly fathered by Barton. Joseph Barton has a community in Digby named after him.
*Whitfield, Biographical, p. 78*

Basteit, John
Digby Township, 1807
Enslaved one female and her child, possibly fathered by Basteit.
*Petition of John Taylor and Other Slaveowners*

Bayard, Samuel (Major)
Wilmot, 1783
Enslaved three people, one male, Cyrus, (age 50), Nell (18) and her 'mulatto' child (seven months).
*Hodges, Book One, p. 118*

Bayer, Family of
Musquodoboit, 1780s
Enslaved one unknown person.
*Smith, p. 25*

Beaubassin, Philipe
Louisbourg, Cape Breton, 1749
Enslaved three persons, including one male, Jean Unique, and one female, Marie.
*Whitfield, Biographies, pp. 188; 119;*
*Donovan, Nominal, p. 149*

Belcher, Benjamin Sr.
Cornwallis/Kentville Kings County, 1800-1802
Enslaved seven known persons; Primer, Dinah, Jack, Prince,
Samuel, James, Cloe.
Has a major street in Kentville named after him.
*NS Archives Kings Probate Records B7*
*Whitfield, p. 152*

Belcher, Benjamin Jr.
Kentville, Kings County, after 1802
Inherited from his father Benjamin Belcher three enslaved per-
sons: Samuel, James and Cloe
*NS Archives Kings Probate Records B7*
*Whitfield, p. 152*

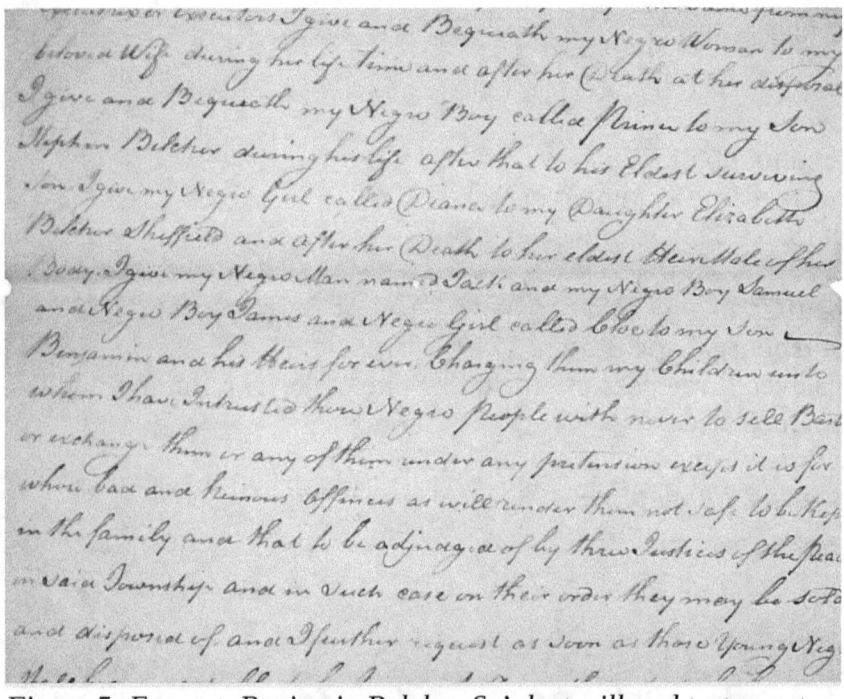

*Figure 5: Excerpt, Benjamin Belcher Sr.'s last will and testament*
...in which he left his enslaved people to members of his family.
Two of these African Nova Scotian people became founding

members of Pine Woods and Gibson Woods, well known Black Communities in Kings County. Both these communities were later negatively impacted when the area was given over to the military and became known as Camp Aldershot.

*Nova Scotia Archives Kings County Probate Records Estate Case File B7 (microfilm 19779)*

Belcher, Mrs. Benjamin Sr.
Kentville, Kings County, after 1802
Inherited 'my Negro Woman" from her husband Benjamin Sr. Possibly she inherited Dinah. No indicators what happened to Primer and Prince after the death of Belcher Sr.
*NS Archives Kings Probate Records B7*
*Whitfield, Biographical, p. 152*

Bellair, Pierre
Louisbourg , 1745
Enslaved one woman, name unknown, whom he inherited from his mother. *See Anne Gyon Despres.*
*Donovan, Slaves, p. 16*

Bennet - first name unknown
Horton Township, Kings County, 1804
Enslaved two adult persons and one female child, Percilla (age 8). Sold all three persons to William Robertson, along with Jane Dickson and William Prince.
*Whitfield, Biographical, p. 141*

Bennett, Joseph (Reverend)
Fort Edward (Windsor), Kings County, 1778
Enslaved one male, name and age unknown.
An American privateer carried off Bennett's enslaved person and he complained about it.
*Whitfield, "Biographical", pp. 81-82, 191*
*See next page.*

"About 1778, his vessel and a thirteen year old black servant boy were taken from him by the Americans. In reporting the incident to the SPG, Bennett valued the boy at £40, and said the losses put him £200 in debt."

*States, quoting L.S. Loomer, p. 40*

Benoist, Charles
Île Royale, 1733
Enslaved one male, Charles (age 18).
*Donovan, Slaves and their Owners, p.8*

"In 1733, Charles, an 18-Year old black slave, produced much of the food consumed in his owner's household. Charles was the property of Pierre Benoist, an ensign in the garrison at Louisbourg, who lived with his family in block 2 of the town. By 1733, Pierre and his wife, Anne Levron, residents of the town since 1722, had two daughters, 15-year old Anne and eight- year old Marie Anne. Maintaining the Benoist household was a full time job for Charles. The courtyard of the property had a garden measuring 34 by 45 feet and three animal sheds housing two goats, a sow, 30 hens and roosters, eight ducks and six turkeys. In addition, Benoist had another 90 square-foot garden in nearby block 22 of the town. When not planting, weeding, harvesting the vegetables or feeding the livestock, Charles would have been busy cutting, kindling and keeping the stoves and fireplaces supplied with wood. By December 1733 the Benoists had 10 cords of wood in their backyard. A prized member of the household, Charles was valued at 512 livres in 1733."

*Donovan, Slaves and their Owners, p.3*

Benson, Christopher (Captain)
Granville Township, 1787-1790
Enslaved between four and six people, including one female and three males: Lydia, John Moses, Dave and Squire.
Squire and Dave were sold in 1787 to an unknown buyer.
*Granville Township Book, MG 4, Vol. 34, Item 3, NS Archives*
*Harris, p. 6*
*Perkins, p. 132*

Betts, Richard
Annapolis County, 1786
Enslaved four people, three males and one female: Harry, Toney, Prince (aka Primus) and Jane.
*see Sinclair, Frederick*
*Whitfield, "Biographical", pp. 81-82, 184*
*Perkins p. 132*

> In the inventory of the will of Richard Betts...appear the following items: one Negro man named Toney £35; one Negro man named Primus £35; one Negro man named Harry £40; one Negro wench named Jane £35.
>
> *Perkins, p. 138*

Bigot, Francis Commissaire-ordonnateur
Louisbourg, 1742
Enslaved two people; François and his wife.
*Whitfield, p. 71*

> "Francis Bigot wrote to the minister of the marine in 1740 asking that a slave from the West Indies be sent to Ile Royale to act as executioner. Acting on the Minister's request, the Superior Council of Martinique selected Francois, a slave who had been convicted of the unpremeditated murder of a small black boy. The court in Martinique offered Francoise the choice of either being executed for the murder or taking the position of hangman at Louisbourg.

> Francoise thanked the councillors and 'voluntarily accepted the said charge'...To ensure that Francoise remained obedient, the Louisbourg authorities provided him with rations from the King's storehouse, paid him 300 livres per year, and, in 1743, purchased 'an English slave' from Simine Millou, a Louisbourg widow, for 154 livres, to become his wife."
>
> *Donovan, Slaves in Île Royale, p. 19*

Birmingham, Richard
Port Roseway, 1783
Enslaved one male known as Sampson aka Bush (age 40).
*Whitfield, p. 167*

Blair, Daniel
Port Roseway, 1783
Enslaved one person, Peggy (age 20).
*Hodges, Book Two, p. 146*

Blanchard, Louis
Île Royale (Cape Breton), 1752
Enslaved one female whose name and age are unknown.
*Donovan, Nominal, p. 158*

Bloss, Thomas (Captain)
Halifax, Sept. 22, 1750
Enslaved 16 persons; names and ages unknown.
Referred to by Governor Wentworth in a letter.
*NS Archives RG1 Vol 35 no. 25 microfilm 15231*

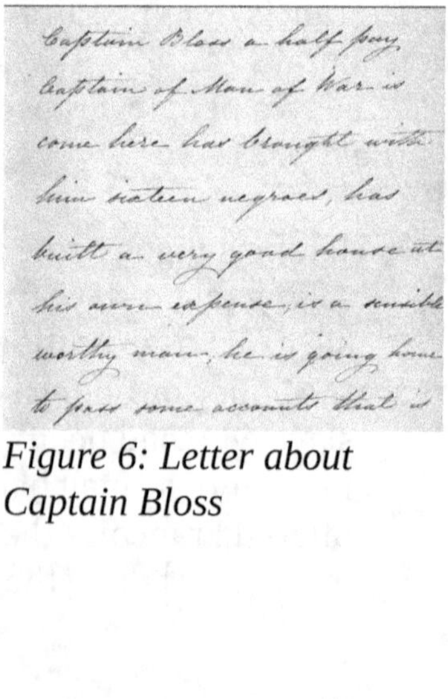
Captain Bloss a half pay
Captain of Man of War is
come here has brought with
him sixteen negroes, has
built a very good house at
his own expense, is a sensible
worthy man, he is going home
to pass some accounts that is

*Figure 6: Letter about Captain Bloss*

*See next page.*

Part of a letter from Governor Cornwallis about Captain Bloss, who brought with him 'sixteen negroes' and has built a 'very good house' using, no doubt, the enforced labour of his sixteen enslaved people.

Bogart, James
Annapolis County, 1783
Enslaved one female and her child. Possibly fathered by Bogart. Sarah (age 20) and her daughter Susannah (6 months).
*Whitfield, p. 168*

Boggs, John
Shubenacadie, 1783
Enslaved one female and her child, possibly fathered by Boggs: Nancy (age 40) and her son David (7) who had learning barriers.
*Whitfield, p. 134*
*Book of Negroes*

Bohme, F.L. (Dr.)
Digby Township, 1807
Enslaved two males and one child. Names and ages unknown.
*Petition of John Taylor and Other Slaveowners*

Bolner, Elias
Shelburne, 1783
Enslaved one female, Letitia (age 25).
*Whitfield, p. 113*
*Book of Negroes*

Bond, (Dr.)
Yarmouth, 1802
Enslaved one female, one male, one child: Kate, Manuel Jarvis, and Hester.
Bond Street in Yarmouth was likely named after Dr. Bond.
*Robart-Johnson, Africa's Children, pp. 48-49.*
*See next page.*

Bond purchased Jarvis (who was from the West Indies) from Col. Lewis Blanchard for £39 in 1801. In 1802 he purchased Kate from the same man for £40. Manual and Kate married and had a child.

*Smith, pp. 63-64*

Bonnell, David & Isaac
Annapolis County, 1786
The Bonnell brothers shared enslaved woman Letisha and her three children Bob, Tom and a third, name unknown.
*Harris, Negro Population of the County of Annapolis, p. 17*

Bonnell, Isaac
Digby Township, 1806-1807
Enslaved six persons; Violet Wells and her three children, Bob, George, John, Tom and one Unknown
*Isaac Bonnell, 1806*
*Annapolis County, RG 48, Probate Records, NS Archives*

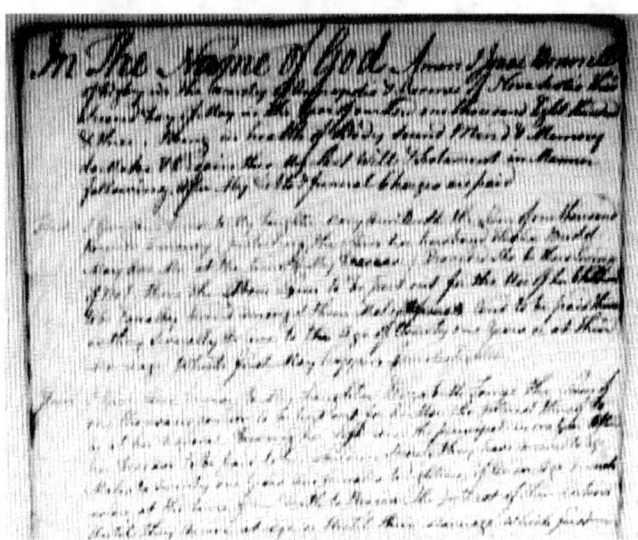

*Figure 7: Isaac Bonnell's last will and testament*

Bonnell expressed his desire to have Bob, George and

John taught to read and to be manumitted.

My desire is that my Black Boys George, Tom and Bob be taught to read distinctly in the Bible and to write a legible hand that they be set at Liberty as they severally arrive at the age of twenty four years. Each to be allowed a suit of good new clothes of every description beside their common wearing apparel. George was born in November, 1790, Tom was born in May 1792, and Bob was born in February, 1794

*uelac.ca/wp-content/uploads/2021/04/Isaac-Bonnell.pdf*

Bonnett, Isaac
Annapolis County, 1807
Enslaved two children, names and ages unknown.
*Petition of John Taylor and Other Slaveowners*

Booth, William (Captain)
Shelburne, 1789
Enslaved two women, Betty Anna and Nancy
*Shelburne County Archives and Genealogical Society, 2008, p. 90-1*
*Whitfield, p. 135*

*Figure 8: William Booth painting of a Black Loyalist, 1788*

One of the two known paintings of Black Loyalists (the other being of Rose Fortune), done by Captain William Booth in 1788.

"This watercolour sketch by Captain William Booth, Corps of Engineers, is the earliest known image of an African Nova Scotian. He was probably a resident of Birchtown.

According to Booth's description of Birchtown, fishing was the chief occupation for "these poor, but really spirited people." Those who could not get into the fishery worked as labourers, clearing land by the acre, cutting cordwood for fires, and hunting in season."

*National Archives of Canada C-040162*
*W.H. Coverdale Collection of Canadiana*

Bosworth, Thomas
Shelburne, 1783
Enslaved one male, London (age 68).
*Whitfield, p. 115*
*Book of Negroes*

Bouisseau, James (Lieut.)
Île Royale, 1784
Enslaved five people: four males, Cato, Charles, Ned, George and one female, Nelly.
*Settlers at Country Harbour*
*Whitfield, p. 73*

"In the early days of the present century there stood on the property of the Barringtons, between North Sydney and Sydney Mines, a building known to have been occupied by the slaves of the original owner - Boisseau, who had brought them from the West Indies."

*Smith p. 33-34*

Boullot, Jean (Captain)
Île Royale (Cape Breton), 1741-1758
Enslaved one woman and her son, Flore Marie and Denis.
*Donovan, "Slaves", p. 150*

Boullet, Pierre
Île Royal (Cape Breton), 1750s
Enslaved three people: Marie Flore, her child, and one other, name unknown.
*Donovan, "Slaves", p. 35*

Bradstreet, Mary & Robie, Hannah Lee (sisters-in-law)
Halifax, 1780s
Enslaved one female, Flora and her son Prince.
Robie originally owned Flora and Prince, but when she died, Bradstreet inherited them.
*O'Brien, pp. 203-206*

Breuff, Charles Oliver
Liverpool, 1784
Enslaved fifteen people, names and ages unknown
*Smith, p. 23*

Breynton, John (Reverend)
Hants County, 1776
Enslaved one female, Dinah
*Journal of Rev. John Wiswall*

Dinah was in her mid twenties when she was sold to Peter Shey of Falmouth for 23 pounds, six shillings and eight pence in 1776.

Reverend Breynton worked at St. Paul's Anglican Church in Halifax.

*See next page.*

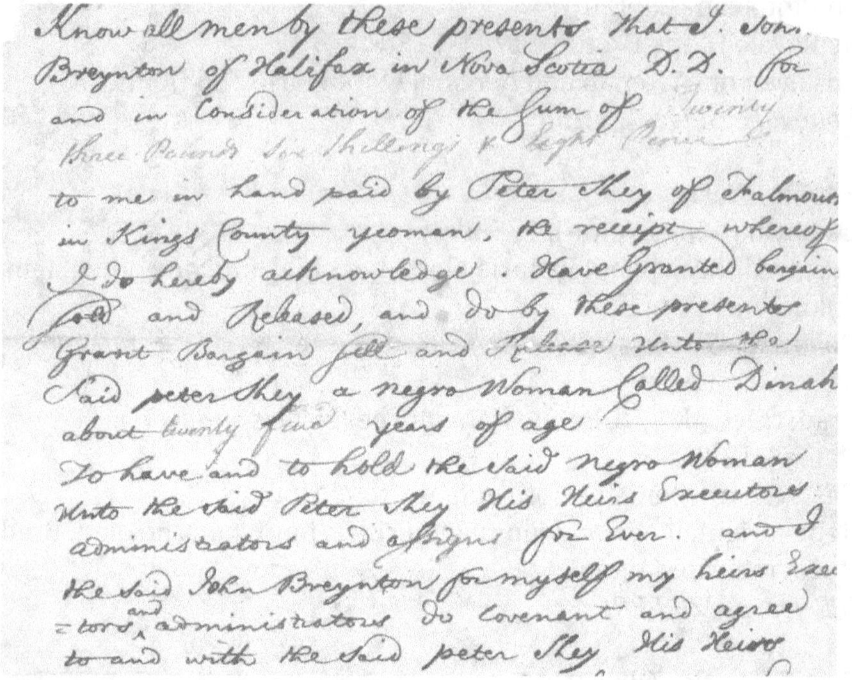

Know all men by these presents that I. John
Breynton of Halifax in Nova Scotia D.D. for
and in Consideration of the Sum of Twenty
three Pounds Six Shillings & Eight Pence
to me in hand paid by Peter Shey of Falmouth
in Kings County yeoman, the receipt whereof
I do hereby acknowledge. Have Granted bargain
Sold and Released, and do by these presents
Grant Bargain Sell and Release Unto the
Said peter Shey a negro Woman Called Dinah
about twenty five years of age
To have and to hold the said negro Woman
Unto the said Peter Shey His Heirs Executors
administrators and assigns for Ever. and I
the said John Breynton for myself my heirs Exec
=tors, and administrators do Covenant and agree
to and with the said peter Shey His Heirs

*Figure 9: Bill of sale for Dinah*
*archives.novascotia.ca/africanns/archives/?ID=12*

Bridgewater, John
Bear River/Annapolis Royal, 1783
Enslaved three people, one known male, Cato (25).
*Book of Negroes*
*Whitfield, p. 38*
*Smith, p. 25*
*Hodges, p. 63*

Briggs, William
Port Roseway, 1783
Enslaved one person, Boston (30) described as ‘stout fellow’.
*Hodges, p. 49*

Brown family
Horton Township, 1780s
Enslaved 'several" people
*Eaton, p. 587*

Brown, Isaac (Chaplain)
Annapolis Royal, 1783
Enslaved five people, Bristol, (age 35), Prince (22), Betty Rapelje (21), Jim (4), Peter (40).
*Hodges, Book One p. 63; Book Two, p.145*

Brothers of Charity
Louisbourg, 1742
Enslaved five people: three males, two females, including Jean Baptiste Etienne, Hector, Jean LaVielle, and Madeleine.

> "In the spring of 1750, Jean Baptiste Estienne, a slave of the Brothers of Charity, attempted to leave Louisbourg on board the vessel Iphigenie. Twenty-eight-years old, Jean Baptiste had worked at the King's Hospital since 1742. A refugee in Rochefort following the siege of Louisbourg, he had returned to Ile Royale with Brother Gregoire Chomey in 1749. Desiring freedom, Jean Baptiste wanted to return to France, but he was discovered aboard the Iphigenie and returned to Louisbourg."
> *Donovan, Slaves and their Owners, p. 17*

Brown, (Major, New York Volunteers)
Annapolis Royal, 1783
Enslaved three people, Peter Huams (age 50), Eli Atken (14), Hagar Buren (44).
*Hodges, pp. 61-62*

Brunet, Jean Jacques
Île Royale, 1752
Enslaved one unknown person
*Donovan, List of Slaves, p. 159*

Budd, Mr.
Digby Township, 1804
Enslaved one woman, Susannah.
*List of Baptisms, September 30, 1804, Records of Anglican Church, Digby NSA*

Bullern, Nathaniel (Dr.)
Nova Scotia, 1783
Enslaved ten people; Achabee (60s), Catarina(60s), Jenny, Prince, Sarah, Dinah, Jupiter, Katty, Nancy & Clarinda.
Jupiter and Clarinda ran away and Dr. Bullern put an advertisement in the local paper for their return.
*Book of Negroes*
*Nova Scotia Gazette and Weekly Chronicle, Sept.21, 1784*

Bulman/Bolman (Dr.)
Lunenburg, 1791
Enslaved one woman, Lydia Jackson.
*Whitman "Biographical" p.93-95*
*Clarkson, Mission to America*

> Lydia was memorialized in George Elliott Clarke's song 'Lydia Jackson', which appears on the *a capella* group Four the Moment 1987 album *We're Still Standing*. Here is an excerpt:
>
> > Lydia Jackson slave madonna
> > Had a master Mr. Bullman
> > A son of Nova Scotia, gave a son to Lydia
> > Gave a son to our Lydia
> > Gave a son to our Lydia

And when she came to him, with the news
He knew just what to do
He beat her, 'till she was black and blue
And their poor son, he died when due

John Clarkson, who led several ships to Sierra Leone, described Lydia's case in an eloquent letter. The passage relating to Lydia begins: "...received several visits from people of every description, one of whom was a young woman a Black named Lydia Jackson. Her case, which I have taken from her own mouth, I shall relate, since it will serve to give some idea of the situation of the Black people in the Province..."

archives.novascotia.ca/africanns/archives/?ID=45

Burbidge, Henry
Cornwallis, Kings County, 1790
Enslaved one male, Spence.
Eaton, History of Kings County p. 234

Burbidge, John (Judge)
MLA for Cornwallis
Kings County, 1790
Enslaved one woman - Fanny - whom he impregnated* and by whom he had several sons. Burbidge enslaved his own children Charleston, Samuel, Job and Jack.
In 1790, Burbidge manumitted his slaves/sons, gave them clothing and taught them to read.
*Eaton, Arthur The History of Kings County, p. 234*
*raped

*See next page.*

*Figure 10: The Burbidge House in Kings County*
From the Nova Scotia Archives
*archives.novascotia.ca/photocollection/archives/?ID=2618*

Burkitt, John
Digby Township, 1784
Enslaved five people; names and ages unknown.
*Smith p. 25*

# C.

Calhoune, Charles
Granville Township, 1783/84
Enslaved three people. Names and ages unknown.
*Perkins, p. 132*

Cameron (Lieutenant)
Country Harbour, Guysborough County, 1784
Enslaved one female, Molly.
*Wilson, Loyal Blacks, p. 181*

Campbell, Alexander
Digby, 1783
Enslaved one female, Nancy, and her son, Tom.
*Whitfield, p. 134*

> "This is the story of Nancy and Tom, who were given away and sold.
>
> On December 11, 1783, 'Alexander Campbell, late a captain in the South Carolina Loyalists, for and in consideration of the sum of forty pounds currency', conveyed to Thomas Green, Esq., late a captain in the Royal Nova Scotia Regiment of Foot, a 'certain Negro wench named Nancy', who, on the same day, 'personally appeared' before Geo. Wm. Sherlock, J.P., and 'freely acknowledged herself a slave and the property of the within-named Captain Alexander Campbell'. Nearly two years later Thomas Green, by a similar document and for the same amount, transfers the said Negro woman to Abraham Forst, gentleman, of Halifax, who one year later conveys, with all his other property, the 'certain Negro woman or wench called Nancy, with her child called Tom', to Gregory Townsend, Esq., assistant naval storekeeper."
>
> *Smith, p. 50-51*

Campbell, (Captain)
Falmouth, 1783
Enslaved one female, Maria, (20 years old)  and her son Mingo.
*Whitfield, p. 119*

Campbell, Colin (Esq.)
Rawdon, 1794
Enslaved one male, James. Age unknown
*States, p. 46*

Campbell, (Colonel)
Port Roseway, 1783
Enslaved 'several' people
*Diary of Simeon Perkins, p. 186*
*Whitfield, p. 213*

Campbell, (Ensign)
Country Harbour, Guysborough County, 1784
Enslaved one male, James Gibline.
*Settlers at Country Harbour p. 24*

Campbell, Roy J. (Rev.)
Yarmouth, 1801
Enslaved one male, Jack. Sold him for £39.
*Smith, p. 63*

Carpenter, Thomas (Ensign)
Nova Scotia, 1783
Enslaved one child, Jack (age 9).
*Book of Negroes*
*Whitfield p. 91*

Carrerot, Andre
Île Royale, 1736
Enslaved one female, Rosalie (age 14).
*Donovan, "Slaves", p. 31*

Carrerot, (Madame)
Île Royale, 1759
Enslaved one one female, Angelique.
*Donovan, "Nominal" p. 160*

Castaing, Antoine
Île Royale, 1749
Enslaved one female, Marie Anthoine Francois.
*Donovan "Nominal" p. 153*

Cassaignolles, Blaisse
Louisbourg, 1734-1753
Enslaved two people; one male, Jean Gassanault, and one female, Catherine. Catherine was purchased from a free man, Jean Baptiste Cupidon, (see Delort, Louis) in order to marry her in 1753.
*Whitfield, p. 72*
*Donovan, "Slaves in Ile Royale", p. 29*

Chalmer, (Mr.)
Shelburne, 1790
Enslaved one male. Name unknown.
*The Diary of Simeon Perkins, p. 51*

Chamberlain, Theopolis
Preston, 1784
Enslaved two males, James and John.
*Whitfield, "Biographical" pp. 96, 106*

Chandler, (Mr.)
Annapolis Royal, 1786
Enslaved two males, William (age 6) and Pomp (age unknown).
*Register of Baptisms, May 1786, St. Luke's Anglican Church, Annapolis Royal*
*Whitfield, p. 232*
*Hodges, p. 45*
Chandler, (Mrs.)
Annapolis Royal, 1784
Enslaved six people. Names and ages unknown.
*Smith, p. 25*

Chandler, Thomas
Nova Scotia, 1792
Enslaved one child, Luke, age 11. Luke was sold by Chandler to Charles Dixon of New Brunswick on January 27, 1792.
*Whitfield, "Biographical" P. 117*

Cheron, Marie Anne Joseph
Île Royale, 1749
Enslaved one woman and her two children: Marie, Marie Jeanne, and Francoise.

> "...Marie Anne Joseph Cheron, the widow of Andre Carrerot who co-inherited a St. Dominique plantation from her brother Etienne in 1752, were women of considerable wealth. The plantation, including slaves, was sold for a net value of 75,000 livres."
>
> *Donovan "Slaves and Their Owners", p. 14*

Chipman, John
Kings County, 1798-1803
Enslaved one male, "Black Peter".
*Whitman, p. 26*

Clarke, Joseph
Digby, 1792
Enslaved the family of Statia, aka Patience (age 30), her husband Richard Hopefield (40), Richard Hopefield Jr.,(5), and an unnamed girl (1). They attempted to run away from him when they lived in New Brunswick.
*Whitfield, pp. 86-88*

Clarke, Samuel
Port Roseway, 1783
Enslaved one male, Jim (age 14).
*Whitfield p. 103*
*Book of Negroes*

Clawson, Jonathan
Shelburne, 1783
Enslaved four people: one male, Pompey, his wife and two children.
*Whitfield, p. 148*

Clows/Clowes, Timothy
Shelburne, 1783
Enslaved two people. One female, Margaret (19 years) and a
daughter (3), name unknown.
*Whitfield, p. 122*
*Book of Negroes*

Cochran (Reverend)
Windsor Township, 1794
Unsure whether Cochran enslaved two males, Daniel Smith and
William, as the Census of 1794 describes them as 'labourers living
at ' Reverend Mr. Cochran's house.
*States ,p. 46-47*

Cock, Daniel (Reverend)
Nova Scotia, 1787-1788
Enslaved two females: mother named Deal and unknown daughter.
*Whitfield, p. 57*

> "The Reverend Daniel Cock, the much-esteemed Presby-
> terian pastor at Truro in 1788, was very greatly surprised
> one day to receive an unusually bulky letter from James Mc-
> Gregor, the young Presbyterian minister at Pictou. The lat-
> ter minister had learned, to his amazement, that Mr. Cock
> had had in his possession two slaves - a mother and daugh-
> ter. The mother, given him, it is said, in Cornwallis, he had
> sold because of her unruly conduct; the daughter, whom he
> seems to have secured by purchase, he had retained. There
> could be no question that these bondwomen were treated
> with kindness; but to young McGregor, recently from Bri-
> tain, where the controversy on the slave trade had begun to
> excite public feeling to its depths, the very thought of a min-
> ister of Christ retaining a fellow-being in bondage was so
> revolting that he made it a special reason for refusing all
> communion with a presbytery tolerating such conduct in
> one of its members.

McGregor next put the letter into the local paper and a community debate ensued. Regardless of who felt what about the enslavement of African people and what Reverend Cock should do, he kept Deal (who became known as Deal McGregor) until his death in 1805."

*Smith, pp. 55-56*

Coffin, (Major)
Nova Scotia, 1783
Enslaved two males and one female: Fortune (age 9), Harry (23) and Nelly (age unknown).
*Whitfield pp. 70-71, 80, 137-138*
*Book of Negroes*

Hodges says he also enslaved Paul Coffin(age 29), Harry, (23) and Phebe (21).
*Hodges, Book One, p.7*

Cole, Edward (Colonel)
Parrsboro, 1783
Enslaved four people, including two females, Annie and Silvia (17 years) and one male, Sharper (aka Harper) Moffatt.
*Esther Clark Wright Archives, Acadia University*
*Whitfield "Biographical" p. 169*

Collins, Benjamin
Liverpool, 1793
Enslaved one female, Rose (aka Pol. Welch).
*Whitfield, "Biographical", p. 163*

Collins, James
Shelburne, 1783
Enslaved one female, Silvia (age 30).
*Book of Negroes*
*Whitfield, p. 171*

Condon, Benjamin
Cornwallis, 1777
Enslaved one man, "my Spanish Indian man servant", who was
then inherited by his son, James Condon.
*Smith, p. 74*

Condon, James
Cornwallis, 1777
Enslaved one man inherited from his father, Benjamin Condon.
*Smith p. 74*

Connecticut Regiment
Louisbourg. 1745 - 1784
Enslaved five males: Simon, Tobe, Benjamin, Abraham & Joseph
*Donovan, "Nominal", p. 156*
*Whitfield, "Biographical", p. 107*

Cook, Robert
Digby County, 1783
Enslaved one male, James, age 19.
*Whitfield p. 96*
*Book of Negroes*

Cornwall, George
Granville Township, 1799
Enslaved three people. Referred to "all my negro slaves" in his will.
*Will of George Cornwall Annapolis County, 1799, RG 48*
*Probate Records NS Archives*

> "I give to my wife Charity, all my negro slaves requesting
> her to manumit and set free by her will after decease, but in
> case they do not behave as honest or orderly servants, I
> wish that she should sell them as undeserving of her or my
> intended bounty towards them."
>
> *Perkins, p. 139*

Cornwall, (Lieutenant)
Country Harbour, 1785
Enslaved one female and one male, Brianna and Joe.
*Settlers at Country Harbour, Loyalist Musters MG 23, D1, ser.1 vol. 24*

Cornwall, Thomas
Country Harbour, 1784
Enslaved one male, Bob.
*Settlers at Country Harbour, Loyalist Musters MG 23, D1, ser.1 vol. 24*

Cornwall, Thomas
Digby Township/Annapolis Royal, 1807
Enslaved one female and her two children.
*Petition of John Taylor and Other Slaveowners*

> "In 1786, Thos. Cornwall of Annapolis Royal, a reduced Captain in His Majesty late King's American regiment, gave to Isaac and David Bonnett, merchants of this place, a bill of sale of one farm, one Negro girl named Letisha, one roan horse named Beatable, one yoke of oxen, and some other articles."
>
> *Perkins, p. 139*

Corasinan, Marie
Île Royale, 1754
Enslaved one female, name unknown, age 60.
*Whitfield p. 224*

Cosby, Anne (nee Winniett)
Annapolis Royal, 1788
Enslaved two females and one male, Agatha, Rose and John Bulkely
*Ann Cosby, 1788, Annapolis County, RG 48, Probate Records, File C 11, NS Archives*
*See next page.*

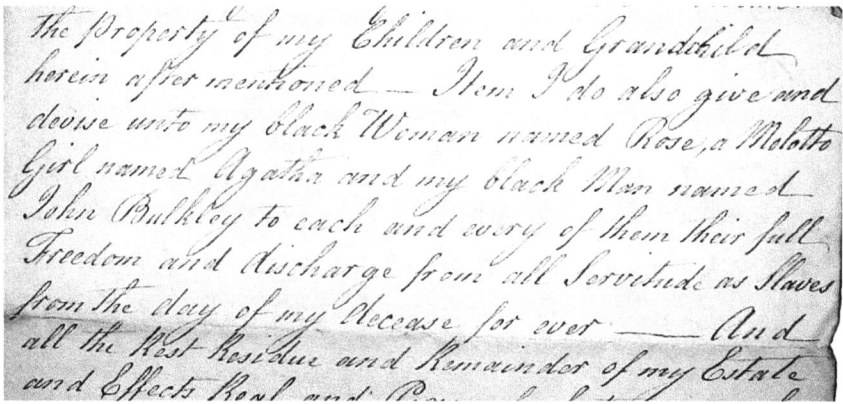

*Figure 11: Anne Cosby last will and testament*

"Item- I do also give and devise unto my black Woman named Rose, a Molotto (sic) Girl names Agatha and my Black Man named John Bulkley to each and every of them their full Freedom and discharge from all Servitude as Slaves from the day of my decease for ever."

Cosby died in October, 1788, shortly after writing this will.

*See next page.*

*Figure 12: The Cosby-de Gannes house, Annapolis Royal*
This house was built over an Acadian cellar in 1708 and is still standing and privately owned. Think of Agatha, Rose and John when you walk past this house.

*Photo by E.G.L. Wetmore.*
*Nova Scotia Archives Photo Collection:*
*Places: Annapolis Royal: Houses:*
*Banks House / negative N-7161*

Cosset, Pierre (Captain)
Île Royale, 1742
Enslaved one male, Arny. age unknown.
*Donovan, Slaves and their owners, p.8*
*Whitfield p. 17*

Coulson, William
Port Roseway, 1783
Enslaved one person, Benjamin (21), described as a 'stout fellow'.
*Hodges, Book One, p. 48*

Cox, James
Shelburne, 1794
Enslaved or Indentured one male, Peter, described as 'young'.

Cox regularly sold the work of his enslaved people to other men. For instance, Cox sold the work of "Peter Cox" to Captain Samuel Mann of the brig Greyhound, which took Peter to Newfoundland and back. Cox sold Peter's work to Zebulon Perkins of Liverpool, who then ran off with Peter to the West Indies. Perkins, in turn, sold Peter to a shopkeeper in Antigua. The case was brought before Nova Scotia Lieutenant Governor Wentworth, who ordered that Perkins bring Peter back to Nova Scotia

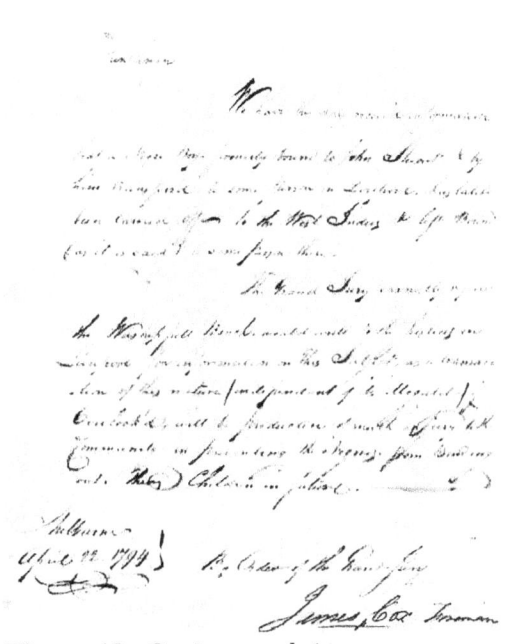

*Figure 13: Cox's complaint...*

... about Zebulon Perkins taking his Enslaved or Indentured man Peter to the West Indies without his permission. April 22, 1794.
*Shelburne County Court of General Sessions of the Peace, Nova Scotia Archives RG 34-321 J 145*

Coxeter, Bartholomew
Shelburne, 1783
Enslaved one female, Mary Anne (age 43) and her daughter, possibly fathered by Coxeter.
*Whitfield, p. 124; Book of Negroes*

Crawley, Edmund
Halifax, 1787
Enslaved "several slaves" by Tamar Cole and fathered by himself
Whitman "Biographical" p. 51

> "By this document [Crawley] claims as his own 'property'
> his Negro woman, Tamar Cole, and all her children born be-
> fore March1, 1783. To Tamar Cole he gives her freedom, and
> at the same time their freedom to the young children she
> may have had since the date named, as these were not born
> under his 'family's care and expense'. But of the children
> born previous to that date he gives one each to four young
> nephews and nieces at Halifax the slaves to be under the
> guardianship of the young people's parents...Each slave
> upon the attainment of that age (36) was to be free upon
> the production of a certificate from the minister and church
> wardens of St. Paul's of good behavior 'as becomes negro
> slaves'."
>
> *Smith p. 59*

Creamer, Balthazar
Preston, 1796
Enslaved one adult female with two male children and two female
children: Mary, Sary, Benjamin and Pompey
*Smith "Slaves in Canada", p. 94*
*Whitfield "Biographical", p. 148*

Creighton, John (Lt. Col.)
Lunenburg Town, 1782
Enslaved one female, Silvia, and one other person of unknown
gender, age or name.
*Whitfield "Biographical" pp. 171, 203*

Croscup, John
Granville Township, 1796
Enslaved one toddler female, Catherine.
*Bill of Sale, Chesley Papers, MG 1, Vol. 177 Doc. 75 NS Archives*
*See Fowler, John for a partial view of the Bill of Sale..*

Cunningham, John
Windsor, 1769
Enslaved one male, Quine, and two females, Flora and another of unknown name. Cunningham took Flora to court for stealing and she was sentenced to 25 lashes to her back.
*Whitfield "Biographical" pp. 155, 193*

"Among the dwellings destroyed at Windsor, N.S., on a fateful Sunday in October, 1897, was one at which I had often looked askance in childhood, because of the story that a slave boy, killed by a blow from a hammer in the hand of his master, has been known to put in an occasional appearance there."

*Smith, T.W. The Slave in Canada p. 77*

"The murderer was John Cunningham, who had served as Indian Superintendent under Governor John Parr from 1769 to 1773."

*Frost and States, Section 3. p. 9*

"The account of Archibald & William Smith, & Joseph Burges of Newport, for aprehending (sic) & conveying Cunningham to jail, who was tried for Murdering one of his slaves and acquitted."

NSA, RG 34-313, P. 1 Court of General Sessions,
Hants County, 30 October 1787

"Quine and Flora a negro women, (sic) were lately tried, convicted and sentenced to receive 25 Lashes at the Public

Whipping Post, for stealing sundry Articles from John Cunningham Esq. And on Saturday last they received their punishment."

*Nova Scotia Chronicle and Weekly Advertiser,*
*30 May-6 June 1769*

Currie, (Mr.)
Country Harbour, 1784
Enslaved one male, John Ambrose
*NSA Settlers at Country Harbour, Muster Master General's Office,*
*Loyalist Musters, 1776-1785, MG 23, D1, ser.1 vol. 24*

Cutler, Ebenezer
Digby Township, 1807
Enslaved one female and her child. Names unknown. Child likely fathered by Cutler.
*Petition of John Taylor and Other Slaveowners*

Cuyler, Abraham (aka Adam)
Sydney, 1792

Enslaved one female, Diana (age 15) with her male child Bastian. Diana died young after she was seduced or raped by George More, Esq, Naval Officer.

Some records indicate Diana was gang raped by More and several powerful men of the area. Diana was pregnant with twins, only one of whom survived. She begged More's brother, a Justice of the Courts, to have his brother admit paternity of her surviving child but he refused. Diana died shortly afterwards.
*Whitfield, p. 19*
*Burial Record 1785-1827, St. George's Anglican Church, Sydney,*
*Sept. 15, 1792*

*See next page.*

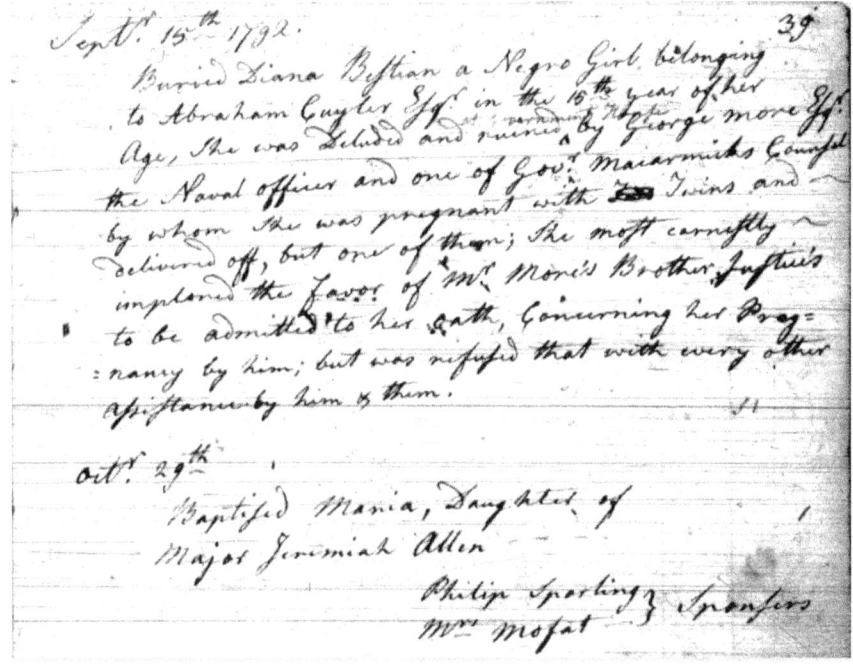

*Figure 14: Burial record of Diana Bustian*
...who was enslaved to Adam Cuyler of Sydney, Cape Breton, September 15, 1792.
*archives.novascotia.ca/africanns/archives/?ID=49*

# D

Daccarette, Michel
Île Royale, 1732
Enslaved two males and one female; Jean Baptiste Cupidon (12 years) Simon Blaise (15) and Catherine.
*Donovan, "Slaves and Their Owners in Ile Royale", p. 101*
*Whitfield, p. 173*

> "Daccarette returned home at four o'clock on a Saturday morning. Upon discovering his slave asleep in the kitchen, Daccarette gave him 'several cracks with his cane' and told him to go out and investigate a noise in the yard...After a

late night, Daccarette's slave bore the brunt of his master's ill temper."

*Donovan "Slaves in Île Royale", p. 22*

Daccarette, Milly
Louisbourg, 1753
Enslaved one male, Touissant.
*Donovan, "Slaves", p. 22*

Dailleboust, Charles J.
Île Royale, 1730
Enslaved one female, Marie Therese (age 15) and daughters Marie Francoise, Marie Angeliquie, and Claude. All fathered by Dailleboust through rape.
*Donovan, "Slaves and Their Owners", p. 152*
*Whitfield, p. 122*

Dalton, Thomas
Port Roseway, 1783
Enslaved one man, Stephen Pottle (age 26).
*Hodges, Book Two, p. 147*

Dawkins, George (Captain)
Country Harbour, 1784
Enslaved two males, William Ransom and Tony.
*Whitfield, "Biographical", pp. 156, 185*

Davenport, Samuel
Port Roseway, 1783
Enslaved one female, Nan. Age unknown.
*Whitfield, "Biographical", p. 133*

Day, Mary (Mrs.)
Annapolis Royal, 1767
Enslaved one female, Louisa, who was purchased from Charles
Proctor by Mrs. Reverend Mary Wood who, in turn, "assigned over"
Louisa to her daughter, Mary Day.
*Smith, pp. 14-15*

de Belle Îsle, Marie Anne
Île Royale, 1733
Enslaved one female child, Catherine Francoise, seven years old.
*Donovan, "Nominal ", p. 29*

de Costebelle, Pasteur (Governor)
Île Royale, 1713
Enslaved one male, Georges. Age unknown.
*Whitfield, "Biographical", p. 74*

Delancey, James (Colonel)
Annapolis Royal/Tupperville, 1794-1804
Enslaved six people. Three females, Nance, Jane and Harriet along
with three males, Charles, Jack and Caesar. All ages unknown.
  Jack ran away from the Delancey home and went to Halifax,
where he became the centre of an important 'runaway slave' trial.
*Whitfield, p. 80*
*Smith, p. 25*

> "Col. DELANCEY was known locally as the Old Major and
> led a plantation lifestyle. He reportedly trained a beautiful
> slave girl to stand still while he shot a turban off her head.
> To entertain his guests after dinner, the girl would appear in
> the garden wearing a yellow turban. The Old Major would
> boast that he could shoot it off her head if he just had his
> gun at hand. Whereupon, Black Caesar would appear with
> the weapon. At a range of sixty yards the Old Major would
> then delight his society guests with a perfect shot. The
> turban would fall, and the girl would be unharmed.

This slave girl was reportedly the Old Major's favourite, and he promised to free her when he died. This happened in 1804, when the slave girl poisoned the Old Major's coffee.

Col. James Delancey is buried in a small family plot in Round Hill, Annapolis County, Nova Scotia, near the tracks of the Windsor & Annapolis Railroad. The inscription on his tombstone says only "Honorable Colonel James DELANCEY/ He lived respected and died universally regretted."

*The Nova Scotia Genealogist, Vol. IX/2 1991*

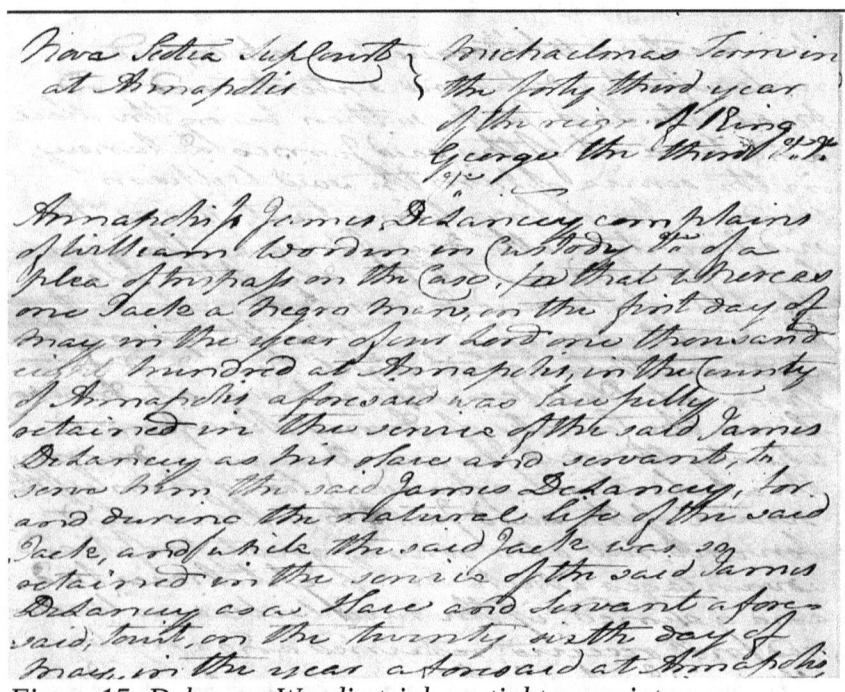

*Figure 15: Delancey-Woodin trial, partial transcript*

"In 1801 at the September term of the Supreme Court, a very important case was tried in Nova Scotia; a slave named Jack ran away from James DeLancey near Round Hill and eventually found his way to Halifax and found employment on wages with Mr. Wm. Woodin. A demand was made by Thomas Ritchie, Esq., on behalf of Mr. DeLancey for the wages of the slave and later an action of trover was brought for the Negro by which Mr. DeLancey recovered a verdict for damages. But the counsel for the defendant, R.J. Uniacke, moved the Court to arrest the judgment that an action of trover would not lie for conversion of a Negro in this province as here he could no more be the slave of Mr. DeLancey or any other person. At the September term of the Supreme Court in 1803 at Annapolis Royal, William Woodin was summoned to appear to answer to James DeLancey on the sum of £500 damages in a plea of trespass. The documents on the file furnish no information to the issue, but it is quite clear that Colonel DeLancey failed to regain possession of the notorious Jack."

*Perkins, p. 143*

"We do know that Jack was not returned to Colonel James DeLancey for, nine months later, Colonel DeLancey was poisoned by one of his female African slaves and died. Jack was not in the list of estate inheritance. "

*archives.novascotia.ca/africanns/archives/?ID=63*

"Mrs. Elizabeth Bailey Bonnett was the granddaughter of both the Rev. Jacob Bailey and Colonel James DeLancey. Included in her silver was a coffee pot that belonged to Colonel DeLancey, the one in which his female slave made coffee and poisoned him. He died from the effects of the poison, in 1804. He had foolishly promised her her freedom when he died and it seems she took this way to be sure of her release."

*Perkins, p. 53*

Delort, M.
Louisbourg, 1743
Purchased two people: one person, "...little Indian named Cola..." but who died during the voyage from Quebec to Louisbourg.
Jean Baptiste Cupidon, from Dakar, Senegal, who purchased his

way out of slavery from Delort then purchased Catherin from Blaisse Cassignoles and married her in 1753.
*Donovan, "Slaves in Île Royale", pp. 19, 29*

Delesdernier, Eleanor
Sackville, Cumberland County
Enslaved one person, Jessie, whom she inherited from her mother, Martha Pritchard.
*Smith, p. 14*

deMolitar (Captain)
Bear River, 1784
Enslaved four people, names and ages unknown.
*Smith p. 25*

deMonton (Captain)
Bear River, 1780s
Enslaved four people, names and ages unknown.
*Harris, p. 7*

DeForant, Isaac-Louis (Governor)
Île Royale, 1739
Enslaved one male, name and age unknown.
*Whitfield "Biographical", pp. 40, 100, 133*

Depensens, Jean de
Île Royale, 1744
Enslaved one female, name and age unknown.
*Donovan, "Nominal", p. 158*

Despres, Anne
Île Royale, 1744
Enslaved one female, name and age unknown.
*Donovan, "Nominal", p. 156*

de Ruis
Île Royale, 1755
Enslaved one male child, Louis Jules, age 12.
*Whitfield, p. 108*

de Sennett, Marquis
Île Royale, 1732
Enslaved one male, Grandcombe, age unknown.
*Whitfield, p. 76*

Delancey, Reed
Shelburne, 1783
Enslaved one male, Joe (age 36), one female, Mary, wife of Joe, and one child by Joe and Mary, name unknown.
*Whitfield, p. 104*

De la Valliere, (Madame)
Île Royale, 1738
Enslaved one female, Marguerite, and her two children, Joseph and Angelique
*Donovan, "Nominal", p. 158*
*Whitfield, p. 118*

De la Valliere, Michel
Île Royale, 1749
Enslaved one female, Charlotte, age unknown.
*Whitfield, p. 42*

Delort, Louis
Île Royale, 1749
Enslaved one male and two females: Jean Baptiste Cupidon, Catherine and another woman, name unknown.
*Donovan, "Nominal", pp. 29, 224*

Denoon, Hugh
Halifax, 1785
Enslaved one female, Phillis, age 30.
Denoon described Phillis as 'having a wart on her nose.'
*Nova Scotia Gazette, Oct. 18,1785*

Denson, Henry (Colonel)
Falmouth, 1780-1783
Enslaved three females and one male: Phebe (age 21), Spruce, Juba
and John.
The community of Mount Denson in Kings County is named after
Henry Denson.
*Smith, pp. 15-16*
*Blacks in Hants County, p. 39*

> "Early non-Planter settlers such as Colonel Henry Denny
> Denson of Falmouth, a former soldier of Irish descent on
> half pay, brought with him a dozen or more slaves. At least
> five Black slaves are mentioned in Denson's will: Spruce,
> John and Pompey, Negro men, Phoebe, Negro woman, and
> Juba, Negro boy. L.S. Loomer informs us that 'Spruce and
> John were sold in Halifax at that time. The estate later sold
> Jube and a man and a woman named Pompey and Phebe.'"
>
> *States, p. 39*

Desages, M
Île Royale, 1755
Enslaved two males, names unknown.
*Whitfield, "Biographical", p. 197*

DesBarres, John Frederick Wallet
Hants County, dates unknown
Enslaved a number of people, two known as "Old Andy" and Cato
Smith.
*Blacks in Hants County, p. 40*
*Whitfield, "Biographical", pp. 140, 174*

Castle Frederick in Kings' County was DesBarres' 8000-acre estate in Falmouth which, according to the 1770 Census of Nova Scotia, took 41 men, 13 women, 5 boys and 33 girls to run. Some of these 92 people were enslaved.

DesBarres was a well known cartographer in Nova Scotia.

From an obituary in the *Nova Scotian* newspaper in 1838: "Death at Castle Frederick, on 8th Feb. Cato Smith, aged 81 years. He was with Governor DesBarres when he surveyed the coast of B.N.A. (British North America) and remained with the family ever since - by whom he will be long remembered for his good qualities, and his death much regretted."

*States, Verna*

"It was said that he was very strict. Colonel Denson supposedly asked his slaves to bury him in an upright position when he died so that he could continue to watch over them. But, as the story goes, they did not follow those orders. They were worried he would come back to life after they noticed his forehead breaking into a sweat three days after his death, so they buried him in the typical manner and placed 10 feet of soil and rocks on top of his grave."

*Thomas*

There are several memorials to DesBarres in Halifax and Bedford.

*See next page.*

*Figure 16: A sketch of Castle Frederick*
by Rev. B.G. Gray, 1932
  *archives.novascotia.ca/photocollection/archives/?ID=5455*

deBrouillan, St. Ovide (Commissaire)
Louisbourg, 1728
Enslaved two children, Jean Baptiste and Charles Joseph (both age 10).
*Donovan, Slaves in Île Royale, p. 11*

Desmaret (Widow)
Île Royale, 1739
Enslaved three people; one male and two female, names unknown.
*Donovan, Slaves and Their Owners, pp. 14-15*
*Whitfield, p. 221*

DesNoyes, M
Île Royale, 1753
Enslaved one female, Mary Anne, and her child, Joseph.
*Donovan, "Nominal", p. 159*

Despres, Anne
Louisbourg, 1745
Enslaved one woman, name and age Unknown

> "Madame Despres had become a modestly successful busi-
> ness woman whose estate sold for 1,453 livres after her
> death in August 1744. Her slave had continued to live with
> her son Pierre Bellair and his family until the day of the
> auction, in March 1745. At 2 o'clock on the afternoon of 22
> March the judge of the Superior Council, accompanied by
> the King's proctor, the court clerk and the usher proceeded
> 'in front of the door of the house of the said Mr. Bellair to
> conduct the sale of a negress belonging to the estate of Ma-
> dame Anne Guyon Despres'. After the drummer had notified
> the public of the auction, and several people had appeared,
> the woman 'was exhibited in public'. In this case, partly out
> of a sense of filial obligation, Pierre Bellair did bid for the
> woman but only obtained her after the sixth bid. Since she
> sold for the small amount of 350 livres, the slave was likely
> a young girl or an elderly woman."
>
> *Donovan, "Slaves and their Owners", p. 16*

de St. Croix, Joshua F.
Annapolis County, 1780s-1805
Enslaved one female, Bess (age unknown) and two males, John and
Newport Tallow. Uncertain if these are the sons of Bess.
*Annapolis County, RG 48, Probate Records, NS Archives*
*Whitfield, "Biographical", p. 179*

> "1814....And if my faithful servant Bess should choose to
> have her freedom, she shall be free and my sons shall pay
> her £10 a year during her life."
>
> *Perkins, p. 139*

Further information on the descendants of John and Newport Tallow is in the very interesting but unpublished document, "Pioneers
of the Mountain", by Janetta M. Dexter, Vol. 1 typescript MSS, MG4,
vol. 293 binders 1-3 in the Nova Scotia Archives.

St. Croix Cove in Annapolis County is named after J.F. de St.
Croix.

*Figure 17: de St. Croix family farmhouse*
...near Bridgetown, where the family settled in 1784.

*Frost and States, Section 3, p. 8*

> "Some of the Tallow brothers took the name 'Tyler' some-
> time between the recording of the 1871 and 1881 Canadian

census, and so appear in records for Inglewood, in Anna-polis County....The Tallows reportedly lived in the area to the west of Hampton Mountain 'near what is commonly called the "Mitchell Field," and were descendants of a man who had been a slave to Joshua T. De St. Crox (sic) named Newport Tallow. Some of the family is said to have been buried in the Mitchel Field.' Unfortunately the exact location of the Mitchell Field is unclear."

*Frost and States p. 20*

*Figure 18: The Mitchell Field*
...still used as a field, is at the western end of Arlington Road, An-napolis County.

*Photo by author, August 2022*

de St. Croix, Pierre
Île Royale, 1757
Enslaved one male, Jacques, age unknown.
*Donovan, "Slaves and Their Owners", pp. 8-9*

Detcheverry, Bernard and Jeanne
Louisbourg, 1749
Enslaved one woman, Catherine Congo, age unknown.
*Donovan, "Nominal", p. 157*

Davoue/Devoue, Frederick
Annapolis Royal, 1807
Enslaved two males, Aesop and Henry Moses (brothers), and one
female, name unknown but believed to be Nancy.
*Harris. p. 8*
*Petition of John Taylor and Others*

> "In the southeast corner of the old Davoue property at the
> Mile-Board* was the family cemetery, now quite obliterated,
> in which there were supposed to be about 30 persons bur-
> ied: Davoues, de St. Croixs, Huguenots, and some slaves."
> *Perkins p. 76*
> *where highway 201 meets highway 8 in Lequille, Anna-
> polis County.

*Figure 19: The last headstone*
...in the Davoue Family Cemetery.

*Photo by author, May 2022*

> "Mr. Davoue 'kept slavery' and brought with him the original Aesop Moses, the first of the long line bearing that name since then to be found in Annapolis Royal. Mr. Davoue's two daughters, Bathiah and Susannah, shared in the amusements of the town and, as their father was very particular with them, they were driven to and from the balls by old "Zip " as a precaution against possible beaux. What did that avail? The young men walked home with the ladies. Zip drove slowly. When he neared the house, he bundled his young mistresses into the coach and on arriving home he reassured Mr. Davoue with a cherry "All right, massa.". The girls in gratitude to this 'shut eyed sentry' compassed him with sweet observances in the shape of mittens, socks, and mufflers. Zip was eventually given his freedom, but such was his attachment to the family that he refused to take it."
>
> *Perkins, p. 77*

Perkins is incorrect about Aesop Moses not taking his freedom. Davoue left Moses 100 acres of land in the Clements township upon his death. Moses built a house for himself on top of what became known as Junction Hill in Lequille where there were other African descendants living in what became known as the local Birchtown. Moses raised his family with other Free Blacks and Indigenous people in his neighbourhood. The foundation and well of Moses' house still exist on private property.

DeWolfe, Benjamin, Member of the Nova Scotia Assembly
Hants County, 1780
Enslaved at least one male, Mungo, 14 years old.
*Whitfield, "Biographical", p. 133*

> "Benjamin DeWolfe....owned a number of slaves whom he freed, but they remained with him....T. Watson Smith mentions that 'Benjamin DeWolf's Account Books show sales of slaves from Hants County in the West Indies.'"
>
> *States. p. 37*

DeWolfe, Elisha (Judge)
Kings County, 1790-1800
Enslaved one female, Phyllis, age unknown.
The town of Wolfville, Kings County, was named after Judge
DeWolfe.
*Whitfield, "Biographical", p. 145*

*Figure 20: The DeWolfe House in Wolfville*
The house is still in existence. Think of Phillis when you drive by
this house. *Photo by Clara Dennis in 1930. Clara Dennis Nova Scotia Archives accession no. 1981-541 no. 409*

DeVeber, (Lieutenant)
Nova Scotia, 1783
Enslaved one child, Kate, age 5.
*Whitfield, p. 109*
*Book of Negroes*

Dickson, Jane and Robert
Horton Township and Annapolis Royal, 1804
Enslaved one female, Percilla. She was sold to William Robertson along with enslaved people Isaac Bennett and William Prince. This was the last known slave sale in Nova Scotia.
Sold to William Robertson along with Isaac Bennett, William Prince. Last slave sale in NS. 1804

> "A conveyance was found not so many years ago in the cellar of the late Peter Bonnett, once High Sheriff of the county, dated in 1804, from Isaac Bonnett and other administrators of the estate of Robert Dickson, late of Annapolis Royal, to Wilbur Robinson and his heirs, of 'a certain negro girl slave named Priscilla, about 8 years and 4 months of age, being part of the personal estate of the late Robert Dickson."
> *Perkins, p. 140*

dit La Floury Thesson, Elie & Simon
Île Royale, 1738
Enslaved one female, Jasmin, age unknown
*Whitfield "Biographical", p. 100*

Ditmars, Douwe (Captain)
Clementsport Township, 1800
Enslaved four people: one female, Eliza, her children Anthony and Eliza, (ages unknown) and one other, details unknown.
*Whitfield, p. 229*
*Smith, p. 25*

*See next page.*

*Figure 21: The Ditmars Inn, Clementsport*
The old Ditmars Inn and Tavern (c. 1816) is on the far right. It is
the only building in the photo that is still standing. Think of Eliza,
Anthony and Eliza Jr. when you drive past this old inn on your
way through Clementsport.

Ditmars, John (son of Douwe)
Clementsport Township, 1791
Enslaved seven people: one female, Dinah (age unknown) and six
other people, details unknown.
    John Ditmars was one of the sons of Douwe Ditmars. John was
eventually committed to the asylum by his father as he was sui-
cidal.
*Baptisms December 19, 1791 Records of the Anglican Church, Digby
Township Book, N S Archives*
*archives.acadiau.ca/islandora/object/research%3A587*
*Smith, p. 25*

Dixon, Charles
Chignecto, 1794
Enslaved one female, name and age unknown.
*Whitfield, p. 228*

Dodd, (Chief Justice of Cape Breton)
Île Royale, 1788
Enslaved one female, Meme Senislohan, age unknown.
*Jan Fralic Brown research papers. St. George's Anglican Church records ANS Mfilm #11912, Vol 5 1785-1813*

Doucet, Amable
Yarmouth, 1806
Enslaved one male, Jerome, age unknown.
*Whitfield p. 103*

Doucet, Harry
Digby County, 1807
Enslaved one man, name and age unknown.
*Petition of John Taylor and Other Slaveowners*

Doucet, Samuel
Digby County, 1807
Enslaved one adult male and one child. Names and ages are unknown.
*Petition of John Taylor and Other Slaveowners*

Douglas, Benjamin (Ensign)
Country Harbour, 1783-1784
Enslaved two males, Dick (age 27) and Nero, and one female, Phebe.
*Nova Scotia Gazette and Weekly Chronicle, Dec. 9, 1783*
*Settlers at Country Harbour*

*See next page.*

RUN away on the 27th Inft. a Negro Man, named, DICK, (belonging to Mr. BENJAMIN DOUGLASS, lateEnfign in the Kings CarolinaRangers) about five feet eightInchies high Stout Made,had on when he went away a red Coatturn'd up with blue, white Waiftcoat and Breeches, Aged about Twenty feven Years. Whoever will apprehended faid Negro and bring him to Mr. ANDREW THOMSON, of *Halifax*, Merchant fhall be handfomely rewarded.

Nov. 29th, 1783.

*Figure 22: Runaway slave advertisement for 'Dick'*
...in the *Nova Scotia Gazette and Weekly Chronicle, December 9,* 1783.

Douglass, William
Port Roseway, 1783
Enslaved one male, Bill, age 25. Described as 'stout ugly fellow'.
*Hodges, Book Two, p. 148*

Driscoll, James
Port Roseway, 1783
Enslaved one female, Nancy VanHorne, age 27.
*Whitfield, p. 229*

Dugas, Joseph & Marguerite
Île Royale, 1733
Enslaved one male, Pierre Josselin, age 25.

"On 20, January 1733...Josselin died of smallpox..." at the age of 25

*Donovan "Slaves " p. 16*

Duhaget, Robert
Île Royale, 1749
Enslaved one female, Charlotte. Age unknown.
*Donovan, "Nominal" p. 157*

Dumoncel, Michel
Louisbourg, 1754
Enslaved two people, Francoise and her daughter Marie Jeanne.
*Donovan, "Slaves In Île Royale", pp. 19-20*

Dunbar (Captain)
Chedabucto, 1783
Enslaved one male with the ironic name of Liberty. Age unknown.
*Whitfield, p. 114*


# E

Earl, Phillip
Annapolis Royal, 1783
Enslaved one male, Peter Lawrence, age unknown.
Peter ran away from Phillip Earl. There is a runaway slave advertisement. *See O'Del(l).*
*Whitfield, p. 139*
*Royal Gazette, July 10, 1792*

Easson (family)
Annapolis Royal, 1810s
Enslaved one male and one female "Black" Charles and "Black" Mary, Thomas Prior/Pryor and Nancy Prior/Pryor.
*Whitfield, "Biographical", pp. 26-27*

*See next page.*

*Figure 23: The Easson House in Lequille*
...outside Annapolis Royal, built 1799. The house is still standing and is a private residence. Highway #8 goes through the back-yard of the residence. Think of Charles, Nancy, Thomas and Mary when you drive by.

*Photo taken in 1972 by Walter Morrison.*
*MG 30, Heritage Trust of Nova Scotia, Series I, vol. 1, no. 1.*

*See next page.*

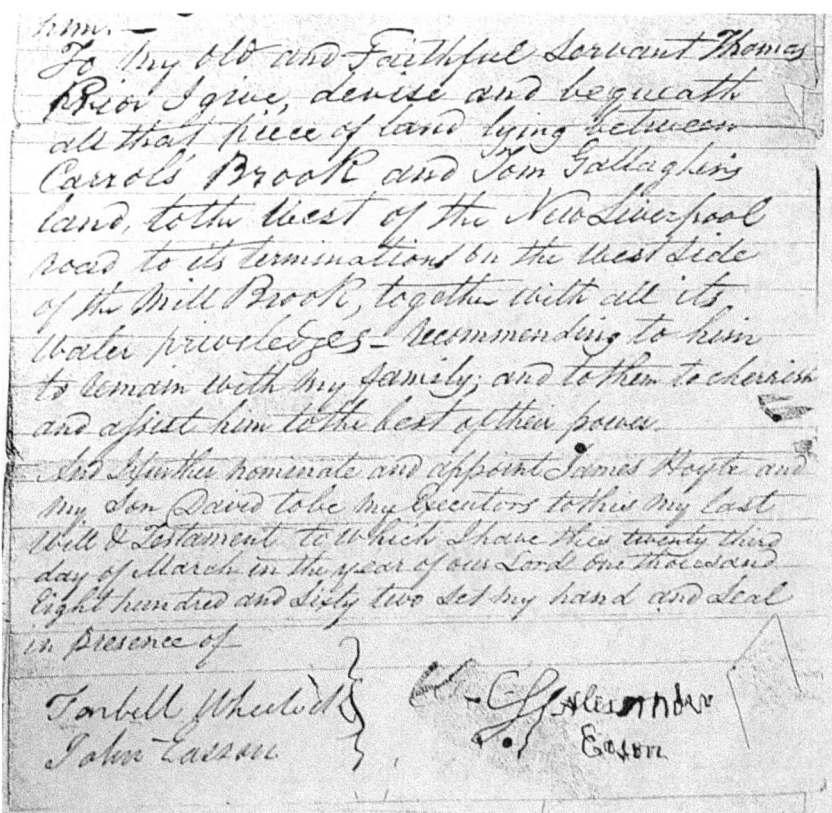

*Figure 24: From the last will and testament of Alexander Easson*
...of Lequille, NS. Although Alexander Easson died in 1862, he refers to Thomas Prior/Pryor as his "faithful servant". Slavery had been over for 32 years by then; however, Thomas Prior stayed with the Easson family. In the will, Easson implores him to continue staying with his family and gives him a plot of land.

Thomas was likely the son of Nancy Pryor, who likely came to Annapolis Royal with Loyalist Frederick Davoue. She passed away in 1827, seven years before the end of slavery in Nova Scotia, so it is likely that Thomas was born into enslavement.

Chute, however, calls Thomas' enslavement to the Eassons into question.

*Chute, Bound to Slavery, footnote p. 101*

Elderkin, (Captain)
Port Greville Cumberland County, dates unknown
Enslaved two persons, names unknown.
*Whitfield, p. 221*

Enslow, Isaac
Port Roseway, 1783
Enslaved one female, Rachel (age 28) and her son David (8). In the
Census of 1827, Enslow showed no 'servants'.
*Book of Negroes*
*Whitfield, p. 156*

Estimanville, Jean B. D.
Île Royale, 1754
Enslaved one female, Marie Anne, age unknown.
*Whitfield p. 120*
*Donovan, "Nominal", p. 159*

Etheridge, James
Granville Township, 1795
Enslaved two people, James Butler and Silvia
*James Butler and Susanna Marriage, 1795, Granville Township Book*
*Whitfield p. 171*

Etteridge, James
Granville Township, 1783
Enslaved one child, James, age 13.
*Book of Negroes*
*Whitfield, p. 96*

Evans (family)
Digby County, 1761
Enslaved two people: one female, Betty, age unknown; and one
'boy', name and age unknown.
Wilson, p. 302
*See next page.*

This may be the same family that moved from Digby County to the Annapolis Royal area.

Evans, Henry
Annapolis County, 1770
Enslaved two people, one girl, name and age unknown and one boy as referred to in the note below.
*Whitfield, p. 193*
*Perkins, p. 131*

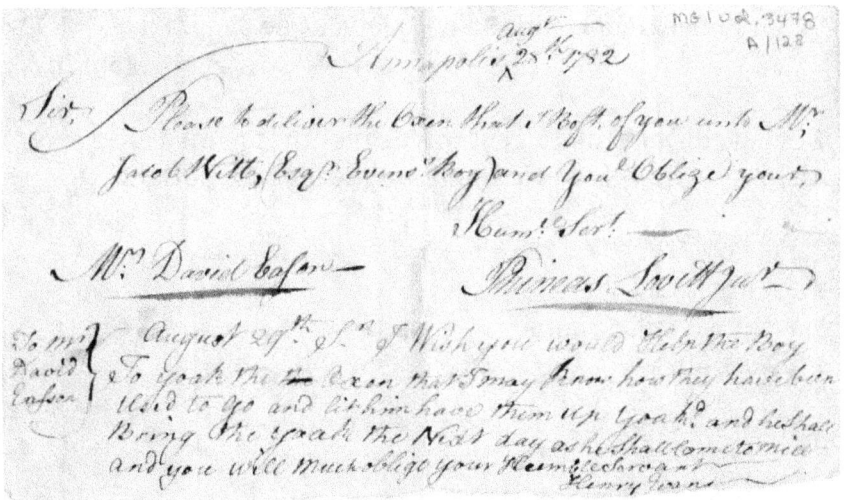

*Figure 25: Note from Henry Evans*
...on August 28, 1782, requesting delivery of the oxen he has bought from Easson, to be taken to Jacob Witt's by Henry Evan's "boy." Addendum by Henry Evans, requesting that Easson show the boy how the oxen were yoked and let him take them away yoked; the yoke to be returned the next day.

*Nova Scotia Archives MG 1 vol. 3478 A/128*

# F

Fairbanks, Joseph
Halifax, 1790
Enslaved one male, Richard Fortune.
*Whitfield, p. 71*

> Fairbanks made provision for the freedom of Fortune in his
> will in 1790, directing that "...my old and faithful servant,
> Richard Fortune, shall be emancipated and made free im-
> mediately after my decease" and made provision for giving
> him five pounds annually so long as he should live.
>
> *Smith p. 84*

It is believed Fairbanks Street in Dartmouth is named after Joseph
Fairbanks, as he was a prominent political figure in Halifax.

Faneuil, Peter
Louisbourg, 1737
Enslaved two males, names unknown.
*Whitfield, p. 194*

Fanning, (Colonel)
Digby township, 1791
Enslaved a female, Mertilla Dixon, age unknown.
*Whitfield, p. 62*

Farish (Mr.)
Shelburne, 1790
Enslaved one male, John Cott.
*Smith, p. 79*

Fautoux, Leon
Île Royale, 1749
Enslaved one female, Claire; and one male, Laurent. Ages un-
known.
*Whitfield, pp. 50, 112*
*Donovan, "Nominal", p.112*

Fergusson, James
Port Roseway, 1783
Enslaved one male, John Kassery (22 years).
*Hodges, Book One, p. 45*

Fisel, Julien
Île Royale, 1756
Enslaved one person, name, gender and age unknown.
*Whitfield, p. 207*
*Donovan, "Nominal list", p. 160*

Fitzsimmons, Peter
Cumberland County, 1783
Enslaved one female, Dinah Simmons, age 40.
*Whitfield, p. 172*
*Book of Negroes*

Flieger, F. H.
Halifax/Cole Harbour, 1784
Enslaved two males, Collins and Stafford, ages unknown.
*Whitfield, "Biographical", pp. 51, 176*

Floury, Simone
Île Royale, approximately 1738
Enslaved one female, name unknown, and one male, François dit
Jasmin.
*Donovan, Slaves in Île Royale, p. 31*

Fordice (family of)
Parrsboro, dates unknown
Enslaved one person, name and age unknown.
*Whitfield, p. 221*

Forst, Abraham (Gentleman)
Halifax, 1785
Enslaved one person, Nancy, whom he purchased from Thomas
Green. Forst then sold Nancy to Gregory Townsend, Esq.
*Smith p. 50-51*

Fowler, Caleb and Mary (wife)
Bridgetown, 1793
Enslaved one female, Hannah, and child Diana.
*Will of Caleb Fowler, 1793 Annapolis Co., RG 48, Probate Records,
NSA Granville Township book*

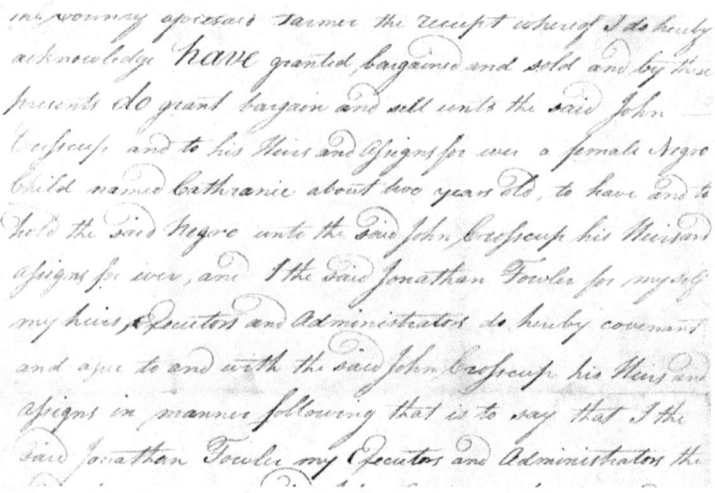

*Figure 26: Excerpt from Caleb Fowler's will*

"Caleb Fowler, of Granville, made a will in 1793...He bequeathed
to his wife, Mary, a Negro wench Hannah and her child Deana, so
long as she remained a widow."

*Perkins, p. 139*

Fowler, Jonathan
Digby Township, 1791
Enslaved one child, Catherine, age 2
*Slave Bill of Sale, Chesley Papers, MG1, Vol. 177, Doc. 75, NSA*

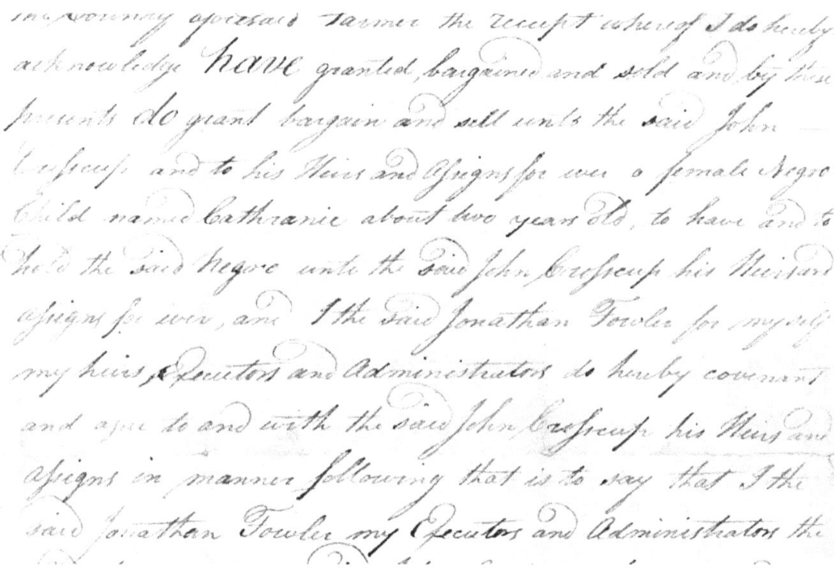

*Figure 27: Excerpt from the bill of sale of Catherine*
..., two years old, from Jonathan Fowler to John Croscup of Granville.

### When We Had Slaves

The following interesting document has been sent to *The Spectator*

Know all men by these presents that I, Jonathan Fowler of the town of Digby, in the County of Annapolis and Province of Nova Scotia, merchant, for and in consideration of the sum of 5 pounds, lawful money of said province to me in hand paid by John Croscup of Granville in the County aforesaid, Farmer, the receipt whereof I do hereby acknowledge have granted, bargained and sold and by these presents do grant, bargain and sell unto the said John Croscup and to his heirs and assigns for ever, a female negro child, named

Cathraine, about two years old, to have and to hold the said negro unto the said John Croscup his heirs and assigns forever, and I, said Jonathan Fowler for myself, my heirs, executors and administrators do hereby covenant and agree to and with the said John Croscup, his heirs and assigns in manner following, that is to say that I the said Jonathan Fowler my executors and assigns shall and will warrant and forever defend in witness whereof I have hereunto set my hand and seal this fourteenth day of July Anno Domini, One thousand seven hundred and ninety-six.
John Fowler
Witness – William Muise

*Annapolis Royal Spectator*, Thursday, October 26, 1939
*Special thank you to Wilfred Allan for bringing this article to my attention.

Fox, John
Cornwallis township, 1783
Enslaved one male child, Jeff (age 9).
*Book of Negroes*
*Whitfield, p. 101*

Fraser, John
Nine Mile River, 1783
Enslaved one female child, Lily (age 12).
*Whitfield, p. 114*
*Book of Negroes*

Fraser, Simon
Port Roseway, 1783
Enslaved three people, John Dunn (age 45), described as 'stout'; Dinah (40), described as 'stout wench'. and a little boy.
*Hodges, p. 48*

Freeman, William (Colonel)
Liverpool, dates unknown
Enslaved one female, Violet, age unknown.
*Smith, p. 19*


# G

Gay, Samuel
Amherst, (Fort Lawrence), dates unknown
Enslaved one male, name and age unknown.
*Whitfield, p. 179*

Gerrish, Joseph
Halifax, 1790
Enslaved four males: John Fame, Cato, Samuel Hazard, Joe.
Gerrish Street in Halifax is named after Joseph Gerrish.
*Whitfield, pp. 67, 81-82*

Gibb, Robert
Port Roseway, 1783
Enslaved one person, Frank Gibb (age 9) described as a 'fine boy'.
*Hodges, p. 48*

Glovers, Robert
Louisbourg, 1745
Enslaved one male, Peter, age unknown.
*Whitfield, p. 142*
*Donovan, "Nominal", p. 156*

Goddard, John
Port Roseway, 1783
Enslaved three people: one male, Scipio (25) described as 'stout fellow"; one female, Effy (23), described as 'stout wench', and a small child.
*Hodges, p. 49*

Gores, James
Île Royale, 1759
Enslaved one male, Jack Griffith.
*Whitfield, p. 90*
*Donovan, "Nominal", p. 160*

Gorham, John
Halifax, 1751
Enslaved one male, name and age unknown.
*Whitfield pp. 206-207*

Grandchamp, Julien
Louisbourg, 1738
Enslaved two people: one male, Asar, described as 'a young black slave', and Louis, a Panis (Indigenous).
*Donovan, "Slaves &", p. 15*
*Whitfield, p. 17*

*Figure 28: Grandchamp houses in Louisbourg*
In this sketch, the two homes in the centre had become the Grandcamp Inn by 1731. Both Asar and Louis lived there.
*Image courtesy of Ken Donovan, "Slaves in Île Royale", p. 15*

Grant, John
Summerville, 1784
Enslaved nine people: Betsy (age 2), Fillis, Harry (7), Maso (9), Nance (28 or 29), Pompy, Sam (13), Peter, and two others.
Whitfield, pp. 23, 69, 125, 133, 166
*States, quoting Edith Mosher and Nellie Fox, local historians of Hants County, pp. 44-45*

> "Edith Mosher of Summerville, NS, wrote in her story 'The Violin Playing Ghost' of her own experiences with Peter, the formerly enslaved man who was still playing his violin this many years later in the attic of her house, the former John Grant home."
> *Mosher, The Sea and the Supernatural, pp.30-33*

Grant, Sarah
Annapolis Royal, 1787
Enslaved two males, Bill and Caesar, ages unknown.
*Book of Negroes*
*Will of Sarah Grant 1787, Annapolis County, RG 48, NSA*

Grant, John
Summerville, Hants County, 1784
Enslaved nine people, names and ages unknown.
*Smith, The Slave in Canada, pp. 93-94*

Gray, Jesse
Argyle and Tusket, 1786, 1791
Enslaved three females: Mary Postell and her daughters, Flora and Nell.
*Shelburne County Court of General Sessions of the Peace  Nova Scotia Archives  RG 60 Shelburne County volume 1 file 49-4*
*Whitfield, pp. 56;149*

> "Jesse Gray, a Loyalist at Argyle, re-enslaved his mistress,

Mary Postell, sold her for 100 bushels of potatoes, and also tried to sell her children back into slavery. Postell complained; Gray was indicted and tried for selling Mary as a slave and kidnapping her elder daughter but acquitted.

Mary affirmed that she had been Gray's mistress and could not prove that she had not been his slave. So she was left in the state of slavery to which he had returned her. The magistrates were Loyalists, many of them slaveholders unsympathetic to the plight of freed blacks who risked re-enslavement at every turn."

*Nova Scotia Archives website: https://archives.novasco-tia.ca/africanns/archives/?ID=46&Page=200402071*

The story of Mary Postell is a clear example of how African Nova Scotians could be free but not free, as they were always subjected to the threat of re-enslavement.

Poet Sylvia Hamilton wrote of Mary Postell:

"Potato Lady"
dusty brown potato
white eyes protruding
she turns it in
her hand, knife poised
and thinks
of Mary Postill
sold
for a bushel of potatoes
*in George Elliott Clarke, ed., Fire on the Water.*

Grayson, James
Shelburne, 1783
Enslaved one male, Samuel Ivey, age 44.
*Whitfield, p. 90*

Green, James
Chester, 1784
Enslaved three people, names and ages unknown.
*Whitfield, p. 214*

Green, Thomas
Halifax, 1783
Enslaved a woman named Nancy, whom he purchased from Captain Alexander Campbell on December 11, 1783.
*Smith, p. 50*

Grenadine, (Mr.)
Liverpool, 1783
Enslaved one male, Anthony and one female, Hagar.
*Diary of Simeon Perkins, p. 211*

Griffith, Robert
Digby, 1783
Enslaved one male, Jack Griffith, age unknown.
*Whitfield, p. 76*

Grigg, Thomas
Annapolis Royal, 1783
Enslaved four people: Mellia Marrant (age 30), Amelia Marrant (6), Ben Marrant (4) and Frank Symons (45).
*Hodges, pp. 56-57*

Grosvenor, Benjamin
Port Roseway, 1783
Enslaved four people: Nancy Davids (age 25) and three small children.
*Hodges, p. 49*

Guest, Henry
Shelburne, 1783
Enslaved one female, Eve (age 64).

*Book of Negroes*
*Whitfield, p. 66*

Gunter, Abraham
Nova Scotia, 1798
Enslaved one male, Joe, age unknown.
Joe ran away from George Dixon in New Brunswick. Gunter took
Joe in but re-enslaved him. Dixon sued Gunter for Joe.
*Whitfield, p. 105*

# H

Haight, Alexander
Annapolis Royal, 1783
Enslaved one person, Nancy, age 23.
*Hodges, p. 148*

Hale, Charles
Port Roseway, 1783
Enslaved one woman, Phyllis, age 14.
*Book of Negroes*
*Whitfield, p. 144*

Haliburton, George
Kings County, 1786
Enslaved one female, unknown name and age.
*Whitfield, p. 226*

Haliburton, William
Hants County, 1779
Enslaved one male, Fillis. age unknown;
*Whitfield, p. 69*
*States, p. 34*

Hall, Peter
Windsor, 1793
Enslaved two females, Dinah and her daughter Violet.
*Whitfield, p. 62*

Hamilton (Captain)
Country Harbour, 1784-86
Enslaved 'several', including Charlotte, Jameson Davis, Lewes,
Phebe Martin, Ranty, Moses Reed, Molly Sinclair, Violet Wells,
James Welsh.
*Whitfield, pp. 42, 55-56, 113, 122-23, 157-158, 231*

Hamilton claimed several people as 'slaves' when they claimed
they were Free. Molly Sinclair and Phebe Martin both testified in
court that they had attained freedom in St. Augustine, Florida but
then were taken in by Captain Hamilton, who did not pay them
wages. Both Moses Reed and Jameson Davis claimed a similar situation, in that they had worked for two years for Hamilton but received no wages. They attempted to escape and run to Halifax to
find freedom and work.

> "At this point Hamilton, along with Captain Daniel McNeil,
> organized what can only be termed a slave patrol, which at-
> tempted to recapture the escaped labourers. The slave
> catchers found the four runaways, put them in irons, and
> locked them in a ship's hold, but not before they beat
> Jameson Davis with a 'Cudgell.' Molly Sinclair recalled 'she
> was Chained to Moses Reed when put on the vessel.' The re-
> enslaved men and women were taken to Shelburne, but be-
> fore they could be shipped away local officials got word of
> their condition and ordered McNeil to bring them ashore
> for an inquiry and court investigation. McNeil claimed that
> he had been told to take the re-enslaved Black Loyalists to
> Shelburne and give them to a Mr. Dean who 'was to give him
> a Receipt for them, and, as he understood, was to carry
> them to the Bahama.' After hearing the testimony of the

four men and women along with McNeil's statement, the Shelburne court considered whether the blacks were the rightful property of Hamilton (there was no evidence such as a bill of sale) or should go free. The majority of the court, five in favor of freeing them and two against, decided that 'the aforesaid Negros' would be allowed to 'go where they pleased.'"

*Whitfield, "The Struggle", page 31, quoting Shelburne Records MG.4, vol. 141, NSA*

*See next page.*

*Figure 29: Country Harbour, date unknown*
*Photo courtesy of Government of Canada, Library and Archives.*
*Thanks to Jocelyn Freeman for showing me this invaluable resource.*

Haliburton, William
Falmouth, 1760s
Enslaved two people, one boy named Fillis and another, name un-
known.

> "William Haliburton, formerly of Boston, lawyer, and Susan-
> nah (Otis) Haliburton, his wife, arrived in Falmouth with
> two Black slaves 'from the household of Mrs. Haliburton's
> father, Ephriam Otis of Scituate.' Florence Anslow informs
> us that 'William Haliburton died on the 20th of February,
> 1817. He had a Negro boy Fillis, who was sent to the West
> Indies in 1779 and sold for £35.'"
>
> *States, quoting Eaton and the*
> *Akins Collection Scrapbook of 1876*

Hardenbrook, Abel
Granville Township, 1784
Enslaved three people; names and ages unknown.
*Perkins, p. 132*
*Smith, p. 24*

Harris, John (Dr.)
Truro, 1786-91
Enslaved three people: Robert Gemmel, Black Jeff and Sambo,
whom he purchased from Archibald Allardice of Pictou.
*Whitfield, pp. 26, 72*

> "During the time Parson Cock owned a black female slave,
> and one or more other slaves were held in Truro, a Baptist
> minister from the United States preached at Truro and
> spoke against human slavery, maintaining that the soul of a
> slave was more precious than a million of money. Coming
> out of the meeting young Archibald* remarked in the hear-
> ing of the minister 'That is strange doctrine you have been
> preaching, for Dr. John Harris bought a slave the other day,
> body and soul, for ten pounds.' This slave of Dr. Harris was

known as 'Black Jeff', who, so tradition says, died of small-pox, from getting up and drinking three pints of cold water when his attendant was asleep'."
*the Honourable S.G.W. Archibald

*Smith, p. 56*

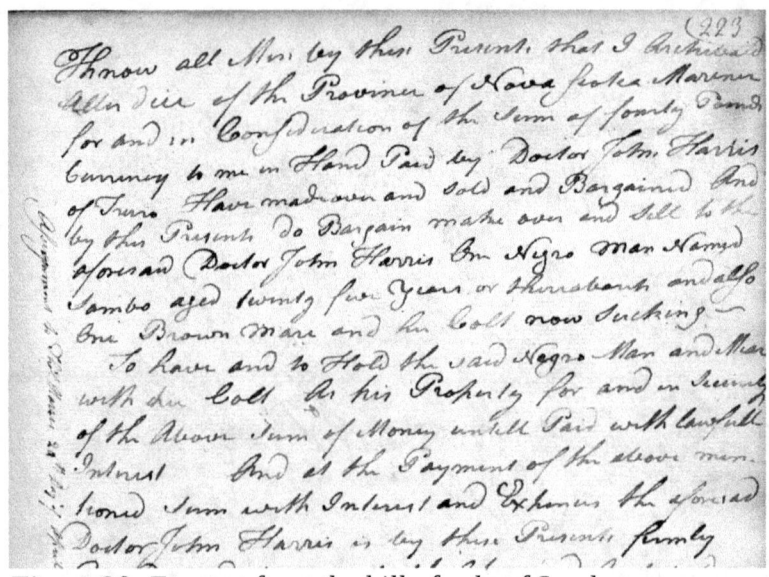

*Figure 30: Excerpt from the bill of sale of Sambo*
...from naval lieutenant Archibald Allardice of Pictou to Dr. John Harris, also of Pictou. Sambo was approximately 25 years of age.

*Nova Scotia Archives Pictou County Register of Deeds Vol. 1A p. 223 (microfilm 18475)*

Harris, Matthew
Brother of John and Dr. Harris
Pictou, 1779
Enslaved two males, Abraham (12 years) and Martin, and one female, Dinah Rhyno.
*Whitfield, pp. 4, 122, 159*

"...a poor woman who belonged to Matthew Harris and obtained her freedom used to confess that her life had never been so free from anxiety as when living with him."

*Smith p. 77*

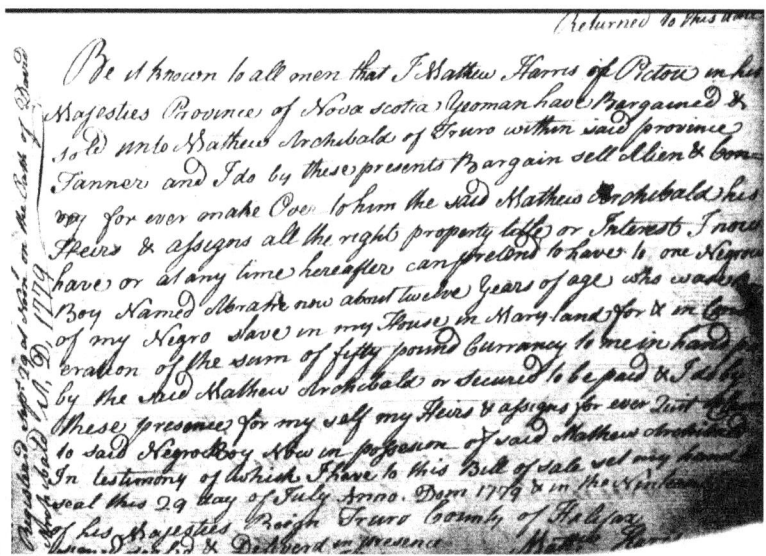

*Figure 31: Bill of sale of Abram*

...from Matthew Harris of Pictou to Matthew Archibald of Truro, at approximately 12 years of age, on July 29, 1779. Abram was the child of one of Harris' enslaved people in Maryland.

*Nova Scotia Archives, Colchester County*
*Register of Deeds Vol.1, p. 468, microfilm 17438*

Hartshorne, Lawrence
Dartmouth, 1780s
Enslaved "up to five" people: Nancy and four others, names unknown.

Hartshorne sold them to Isaac Allen, who immediately set them free. Hartshorne also became an abolitionist and eventually freed all his 'servants'.
*Whitfield, p. 225*

111

Hatfield (family)
Parrsboro, dates unknown
Enslaved an unknown number of people.
*Whitfield, p. 221*

*Figure 32: Parrsboro blockhouse and harbour, 1838*
*Nova Scotia Archives Documentary Art Collection: 1979-147.262*

Hatfield, Isaac
Digby/Annapolis Counties, 1807
Enslaved five males and two females. Only one name is known, that of Nelly, as she is noted as having died of pleurisy.
*Petition of John Taylor and Others 1807*

Hatfield, James
Digby Township, 1784
Enslaved three people, names and ages unknown.
*Smith, p. 25*

Hathaway (family)
Parrsboro, dates unknown
Enslaved an unknown number of people.
*Whitfield, p. 221*
Haynes, Bartholomew
Nova Scotia, 1783
Enslaved one woman known as Jane. Age unknown.
*Whitfield, p. 99*
*Book of Negroes*

Hecht, (possibly Frederick William)
Digby/Annapolis, 1788
Enslaved two females, Bathsheba and Hagar, and one child, Rachel
Bross. Rachel was baptized on November 23, 1788 in the Anglican
Church, Digby.
*Whitfield, p. 18*

Henderson, James
Halifax, 1783
Enslaved one male, Gilbert Lafferts, age 21.
*Book of Negroes*
*Whitfield, p. 112*

Hendricks, Conrad
Cumberland County, 1783
Enslaved one female, Betty, age 20, and her infant child.
*Book of Negroes*

Herbert, John
Shelburne, 1783
Enslaved 'several', including Charles (age 50), David (5), Hanna
(40), Isaac (11), Jenny (9), London (30), Rose (45), and Venus (16);
all with the surname Herbert.
*Whitfield, pp. 83-85*

*See next page.*

"John Herbert, of Shelburne, in a will recorded in March 1799, gave and bequeathed to his wife, Sarah Herbert, a Negro woman named Venus; and to his "son Thomas the house I now live in, as also all the land and lots I hold in the township of Shelburne," and "to my said son Thomas a slave named Isaac".

*Smith p. 62*

Hicks, John
Granville Township, 1784
Enslaved six people, names and ages unknown.
*Smith p. 24*

Hildrith, Isaac
Port Roseway, 1783
Enslaved two people, Prince Augustus (age 50), described as 'feeble old fellow', and Thomas Britton (30).
*Hodges, p. 69*

Hill, Charles
Shelburne, 1791
Enslaved one male, Sam (age 20).
*Whitfield, p. 117*
*Royal Gazette, July 12, 1791*

Hill, Richard
Digby Township, 1784
Enslaved five people, names and ages unknown.
*Smith p. 25*

Hodgson, (Lieutenant)
Country Harbour, 1806
Enslaved one male, name and age unknown. Sold the enslaved man to James Morris. *See the letter under the Morris entry.*
*Whitfield, p. 200*

Holmes, Joseph
Shelburne, 1783
Enslaved one male, Sam, age 26.
*Whitfield, p. 165*

Hornbrook (Captain)
Nova Scotia, 1783
Enslaved one male, an infant named Cato.
*Whitfield, p. 61*

Houghten, Jane
Digby, 1780s
Enslaved six people, names unknown.
*Harris, p. 7*

Houseal, Michael
Cole Harbour, 1784
Enslaved four males, Barny, Caesar, Cyrus and Harry.
*Whitfield, pp. 18, 81*

Hubbard, Nathaniel (Ensign)
Annapolis Royal, 1783
Enslaved Rachel (age 39), children 10, 6, and 2 years old, and one
male, Ham, age 15.
*Hodges, p. 118*

Hubbill, Nathan
Chedabucto, 1784
Enslaved one male, Anthony Bertram.
*Whitfield, p. 22*

Hudson, Joel (Lieutenant)
Country Harbour, 1784
Enslaved one female, Sally and one male, Hercules.
*Whitfield, pp. 85, 164*

Hufton, (Captain)
Île Royale, 1746
Enslaved one male, Rubin.
*Whitfield, p. 163*

Hughstone, James
Digby, 1784
Enslaved six people, names and ages unknown.
*Smith, p. 25*

Hunter, David
Windsor, 1789
Enslaved one man, Juba Hunter.

> "...in which Juba Hunter, A Negro man belonging to David
> Hunter, Planter husbandman, of Windsor, was charged with
> 'feloniously stealing taking and carrying away on the 20th
> day of August 1789 one eye sheep and one lamb the prop-
> erty of Alexander Scott, value twenty three shillings...In
> later years, Juba Hunter, also known as 'Black Jube', ap-
> peared in the Windsor Township Book, in the records of the
> Overseers of the Poor, being bound out to the lowest bidder
> for the following years: April 1825 - Fanny Thompson,
> November 1825 - John Anderson, November 1826 - Hugh
> Frizzle, April 1827-Hugh Frizzle, November 1827 - Hugh
> Frizzle, April 1828- Hugh Frizzle, November 1828 - Mrs.
> Card."
>
> *States pp. 38-39*

Hurd, David
Shelburne, 1791
Enslaved one male, Richard.
*Whitfield, p. 160*

Hurd, Jacob
Nova Scotia, 1773
Enslaved one male, Cromwell.
*Whitfield, p. 52*

Howse (House), Francis
Port Roseway, 1783
Enslaved one female, Eve, age 56.
*Whitfield, p.66*

Hunter, David
Windsor, 1789
Enslaved one male, Jube (aka Juba) Hunter.
*Whitfield, p. 89*
*Blacks in Hants County pp. 38-39*

*Figure 33: Sketch of Windsor, 1854*
*Courtesy of Canada Collection*
*recherche-collection-search.bac-lac.gc.ca/eng/Home/Search?*
*q=Windsor%20NS&DataSource=Images*

Huston, John
Cornwallis, 1787
Enslaved one male, Pomp.
*Smith, "The Slave in Canada", p. 16*

# I

Inglis, Charles (Right Reverend/Bishop)
Halifax, 1773-1778
Enslaved at least two men, Dick (age 19) and Prymis (age 15).
Inglis was the founder of what became The University of King's College.

TWENTY SHILLINGS Reward.

ABSENTED himself from his Master, living in Hanover-Square, the 2d Inst. a Negro Man called DICK, aged 19 Years. He had on when he went away, a Beaver Hat, smartly cocked, a new light coloured Coat and Waistcoat, with Metal Buttons, green Linings, the Collar and Cuffs of the Coat turned up with Green; new Buckskin Breeches, a Pair of ribbed Stockings of a mixed Colour, and Silver Buckles in his Shoes. He is a likely, well-made Fellow, and speaks both English and Dutch. It is supposed that he has been seduced by bad Company during the late Holydays; and that he is lurking somewhere in the City, or its Environs. Whoever secures the said Negro, so that the Subscriber may have him again, shall receive Twenty Shillings Reward, from         CHARLES INGLIS.

*Figure 34: Ad regarding Bishop Inglis' runaway slave, 1778*
From an unknown Halifax newspaper.

*See next page.*

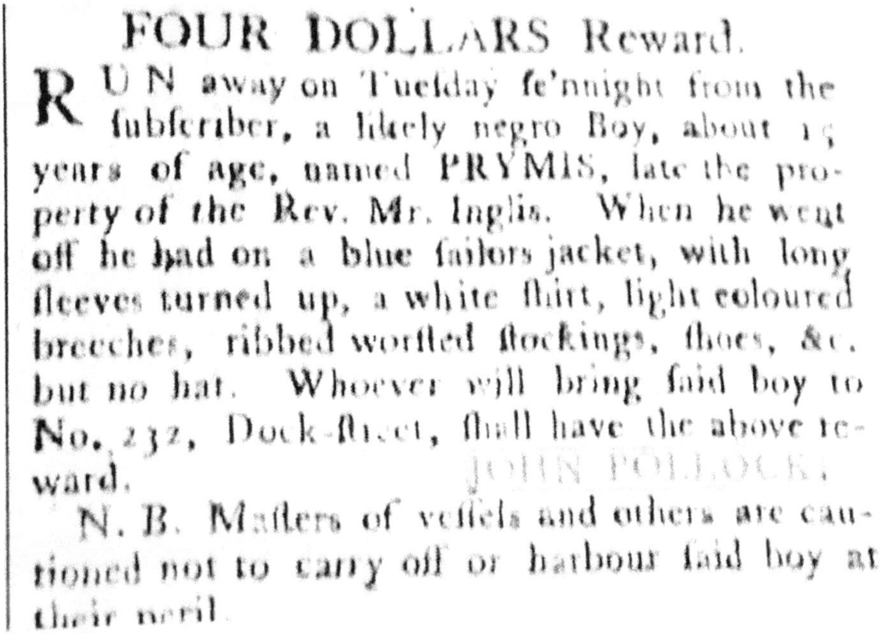

FOUR DOLLARS Reward.

RUN away on Tueſday ſe'nnight from the ſubſcriber, a likely negro Boy, about 15 years of age, named PRYMIS, late the property of the Rev. Mr. Inglis. When he went off he had on a blue ſailors jacket, with long ſleeves turned up, a white ſhirt, light coloured breeches, ribbed worſted ſtockings, ſhoes, &c. but no hat. Whoever will bring ſaid boy to No. 232, Dock-ſtreet, ſhall have the above reward. JOHN POLLOCK.

N. B. Maſters of veſſels and others are cautioned not to carry off or harbour ſaid boy at their peril.

*Figure 35: Ad regarding another of Bishop Inglis' slaves*
*From an article in The Signal Newspaper of Kings' College, Jan. 28, 2020 by Andrea McGuire //signalhfx.ca/founder-of-university-of-kings-college-was-a-slave-owner-says-scholarly-inquiry/*

Irwin, James
St. Mary's Bay, Digby County, 1783
Enslaved one female, Margaret, age 15.
*Whitfield, p.122*

## J

Jakeways, John
Port Roseway, 1783
Enslaved one male, Simon, age 12.
*Whitfield, p. 172*
*Hodges, Book One, p. 49*

Jackson, Robert
Halifax County, 1784
Enslaved one female, Sarah, age unknown.
*Whitfield, p. 168*

James, Benjamin
Granville Township, 1790
Enslaved one female child, Bella, one year old.
*Whitfield, p. 19*

James, Elizabeth
Digby/Annapolis, 1807
Enslaved one male, unknown name or age.
*Petition of John Taylor and Other Slaveowners*

James, Nicholas
Digby/Annapolis, 1807
Enslaved one adult and three children, names unknown.
*Petition of John Taylor and Other Slaveowners*

Jenkins, Richard
Shelburne, 1783-84
Enslaved one female -Dinah or Diana - and two males, George (age 14) and Cato.
*Whitfield pp. 58, 74*

Jones, Edward
Clements township, 1791
Enslaved one female, Dinah aka Sinah.
*Whitfield, p. 62*

Jones, Mariannah
Shelburne, 1783
Enslaved one female, Fanny (age 22), described as 'sickly'.
*Whitfield, p. 68*
*Book of Negroes*

Jones, Simeon
Digby/Annapolis, 1807
Enslaved two people, names unknown
*Petition of John Taylor and Other Slaveowners*

Jouet, Louis
Louisbourg, 1742
Enslaved "numerous" people, including Antoine Francois (born in 1749), Frank, Marie-Louise, Jean Baptiste (son of Marie Louise), Isabelle (daughter of Marie Louise, Jacques, Marie Jeanne, Catherine, Jean Pierre, and Jean Charles.

Marie Louise (18 years) was purchased from Jouet by a white man and former indentured servant, Louis Coustard (25), who then married her.
*Donovan, "Slaves of Île Royale", pp. 30, 154*
*Whitfield, pp. 16, 95, 121*

# K

Kane, (Mrs.)
Annapolis Royal, 1784
Enslaved three people; name and ages unknown.
*Smith, p. 25*

Killo, Robert
Halifax, 1789
Enslaved one female, a 'negro girl' he purchased from Captain John Grant.
*Smith, p. 54*

Kipp, (Captain)
Nova Scotia, 1783
Enslaved one male, Israel Merritt, age 25.
*Whitfield, p. 125*
*Hodges, p. 56*

Kirkham, Hugh
Halifax, 1783
Enslaved one male, Peter., age unknown.
*Whitfield, p. 142*

Knapp/Knepp, (Captain)
Nova Scotia, 1783
Enslaved one woman, Dinah(age 29), and her children, Alice (6)
and Job (1). Possibly fathered by Knapp.
*Whitfield, pp. 111-112*
*Hodges, p. 56*

# L

Lachaume, Louis
Louisbourg, 1734
Enslaved at least one person, Cesard, 12 years old.

> "On 10 November 1734,...12-year-old Cesard found himself
> with a new master on an unfamiliar shore when his owner,
> Captain Charles LeRoy struck a bargain with a merchant,
> Louis Lachaume. According to the sale agreement,
> Lachaume "inspected and was content" with Cesard for the
> price of 350 livres."
>
> *Donovan, Slaves and Their Owners, p. 8*

Larcher, Nicholas
Île Royale, 1758
Enslaved one female, Anne Honiche Nanon, age 24.
*Whitfield, p. 13*

Larreguy, Bertrand
Île Royale, 1736
Enslaved one male, Malfich, age unknown.
*Donovan, "Nominal", p. 158*
*Whitfield, p. 118*

Lartigue, Joseph (Councillor)
Île Royale, 1732
Enslaved one male, Pompee, age 12. Pompeii died that year and
'had been baptized during his sickness'.
*Donovan, "Slaves", p. 13*

*Figure 36: Where Pompee died of smallpox*
...in this building in Louisbourg in March, 1732.

Latigue, (Madame)
Île Royale, 1749
Enslaved one person, Clorin.
*Whitfield, p. 50*

Law, (family of)
Parrsboro, dates unknown
Enslaved an unrecorded number of people.
*Whitfield, p. 222*

Lawson, Sarah
Halifax, 1779-80
Enslaved one male, Adam, whom she inherited from her father,
teacher Daniel Shatford.
*Smith, p. 14*

LeCoutre, Charles
Île Royale, 1753
Enslaved one male, Phillipe, age unknown.
*Whitfield, p. 144*
*Donovan, "Slaves Ille Royale", p. 159*

Leggett, John (Captain)
Country Harbour, 1784
Enslaved seven people, including Michael, Phillis and her daughter
Dinah.
*Whitfield, pp. 126-127, 214*

*Figure 37: Site of John Leggett's house, Country Harbour*
*Photo by Clara Dennis.*
*Nova Scotia Archives 1981-541 no. 275*

Lent, John
Shelburne, 1783
Enslaved two males, William and Berry; one female, Dinah; and one child, Hester MacKinnon.
*Robart-Johnson, Africa's Children, p. 141*

Lagrange, Jean
Île Royale, dates unknown
Enslaved one unknown person.
*Donovan, "Slaves in Île Royale", p. 31*

LaGrois, Louis and wife Magdelaine Morin
Île Royale, 1755
Enslaved one female, Louise, age 20, and her daughter Jeanne Josephe.
*Whitfield, p. 116*
*Donovan, "Slaves in Ile Royale", p. 20*

LeNeuf, LaVallière, Louis
Île Royale, 1758
Enslaved one female, unknown name and age.
*Donovan, "Nominal", p. 160*

Lent, James (Judge)
Tusket Village, 1784
Enslaved William and Dinah Berry and their daughter, who lived to be 106 years old.
*Smith, p. 64*

Leonard, (family of)
Parrsboro, dates unknown
Enslaved an unknown number of people.
*Whitfield, p. 222*

Leonard, Thomas
Kings County, 1788
Enslaved one female, Phillis, and her unnamed child,
*NSA, Probate Records, RG48, Kings County 1788*

> "Leonard made arrangements for the manumission of Phil-
> lis in his will of 1789: 'I give and bequeath to my former
> Negro woman Phillis (I have given her freedom with her
> child) fifty pounds Nova Scotia currency to be paid her as
> follows, viz: Ten pounds in three months after my decease
> and ten pounds a year for four years after, making the said
> fifty pounds.'"
>
> *Smith, The Slave in Canada, p. 84*

LeRay, Jacques
Île Royale, 1736
Enslaved one child, Jacques, age 12.
*Whitfield, p. 96*

LeRoy, Charles (Captain)
Île Royale, 1734
Enslaved one child, Cesar, age 12.
*Whitfield, p. 39*

LeVasseur, M
Île Royale, 1733
Enslaved one male, name unknown.
*Donovan, Minimal List, p. 153*

Lillie, Anna (aka Ann Lilie)
Halifax, 1789
Enslaved one male, Caesar, age unknown.
*Whitfield, p. 35-36*

> Lillie made arrangements in her will to manumit Cesar after
> her death:

"Thus in 1789 Anna Lillie of Halifax, widow of Theophilus Lillie, in her will arranges that at her death her '...black man Caesar" is to be free, and leaves ten pounds with her executors to be used 'in case of sickness or other necessity.' She also leaves him his bed and bed clothing."

*Smith, p. 84*

Longstreet, John (Captain)
Parrsboro, 1783
Enslaved one female, Phillis, age 15.
*Whitfield, p. 144*

Loosely, Charles
Shelburne, 1789
Enslaved two males, Jack Loosely and an 'indentured' servant.
*Whitfield, p. 115*
*Book of Negroes*

Loppinot, Jean (Officer)
Louisbourg, 1736
Enslaved one female, Rose Marie Marguerite, age 19, and her son, unknown name and age.
*Whitfield, p. 163*

"Marie Marguerite Rose, was a native of Guinea and a slave of Louisbourg officer Jean Chryststome Loppinot. Purchased in 1736, Marguerite was baptized on 17 September and was described as being 'around 19 years old'. Two years later, she gave birth to a son, Jean Francoise, who automatically became a slave, the father being listed as 'unknown'...After the capture of Louisbourg in 1745, Marguerite Rose and her son went to Rochefort with the Loppinots, returning with the family to Ile Royale in 1749. Two years after their return to Cape Breton, Marguerite's son, Jean Francoise...died just 11 days after his 13th birthday....Marguerite obtained her freedom sometime before her wedding in 1755. On 27 November 1755, Marguerite Rose was married to Jean Baptiste Laurent, who was described as an "indian" on his marriage certificate...She and Jean Baptiste established a tavern in their Block 16 house and appear to have been equal partners in the business...The marital bliss of Marguerite and Jean Baptiste was to be short lived, since Marguerite died in 1757, less than two years after her marriage."

*Donovan, "Slaves in Île Royale", pp. 28-29*

Lovitt, Andrew
Yarmouth. 1765
Enslaved two people, names and ages unknown.
*Whitfield, p. 209*

Lowerhele/Lowerheli, (Mrs.)
Port Roseway, 1783
Enslaved one male, Jack Dunlop.
*Whitfield, p. 64*

Louisbourg Hospital
Louisbourg, 1726
Enslaved four people: Jean Baptiste Estienne, Madeleine, Hector and Jean LaVielle.
*Donovan, Slaves and Their Owners in Île Royale, p. 17*

*See next page.*

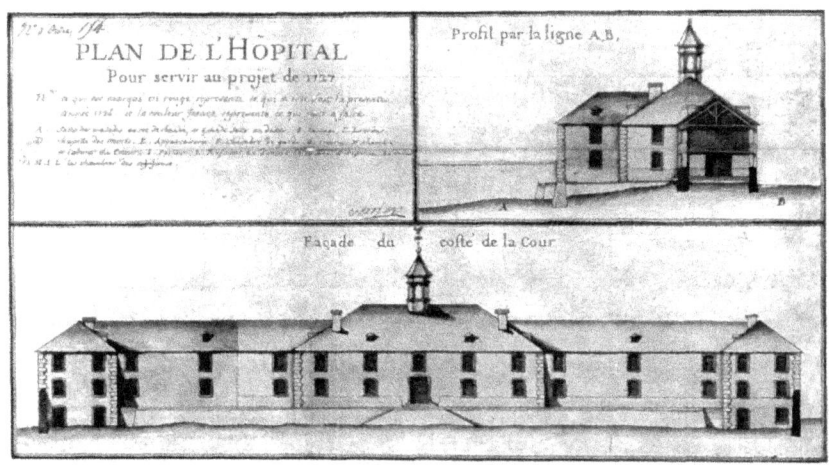

*Figure 38: The hospital at Louisbourg, 1726*
... where Jean Baptiste and the others lived and were enslaved.
*Image courtesy of Donovan, "Slaves and Their Owners", p. 17*

Lumbert, Samuel (Captain)
Louisbourg, 1745
Enslaved one male, Cuffee.
*Whitfield, p. 53*

Lynch, Peter
Halifax and Annapolis Royal, 1783
Enslaved four people: Tinnia Lynch (25 years), Joseph Skinner
(35), Casar Handell, (34) and one child, Sally (6).
*Whitfield pp. 118, 174*
*Hodges, p. 44*

Lyle, James
Shelburne & Chedabucto, 1784
Enslaved one male, Liberty, and two females Sarah and her daughter, Peg. All ages unknown.
*Whitfield, pp. 114, 169*

"Several documents in relation to the last three, registered
in Guysborough County in 1793 by David Martin, show that

James Lyle had in the previous February paid seventy pounds sterling for them in St. Augustine, and that the man had been previously a slave in Georgia, the woman and child slaves in East Florida."

*Smith, p. 26*

# M

James MacDonald (Captain)
Halifax , 1786
Enslaved at least one male, Tom. Tom ran away from MacDonald, who put out the ad on the next page for him. Unfortunately, the newspaper crumbled and tape was put across it.

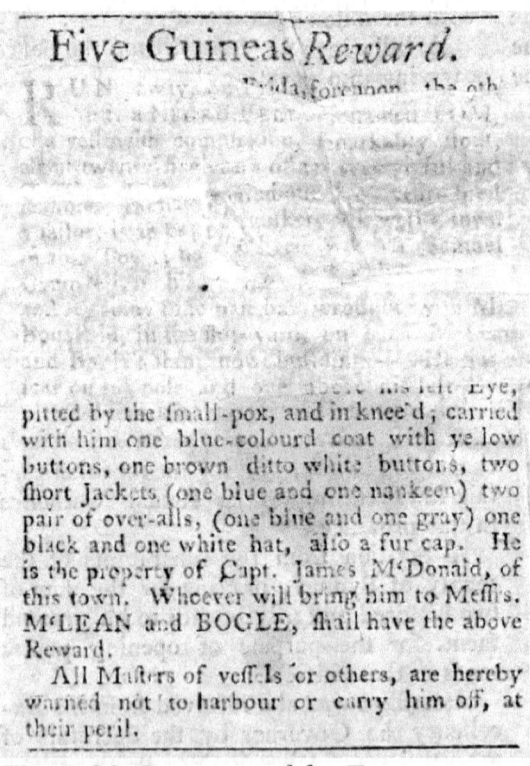

*Figure 39: Runaway ad for Tom*

> Five Guineas Reward. RUN away on Friday forenoon the 9th inst, a NEGRO FELLOW, named TOM, of a yellowish complexion, remarkably stout, about twenty-five years of age, very [artful?] and [...?...] a sailor, is an ex[?] [...in the Town; ha...?] [...with? Mr. Boushelid?], in the ship-yard, [...?] [McLean?] and Bogle's ship, now building [...?...] has a scar on his [nose?] and one above his left Eye, pitted by the small-pox, and in knee'd; carried with him one blue-colourd coat with yellow buttons, one brown ditto white buttons, two short Jackets (one blue and one nankeen) two pair of overalls, (one blue and one gray) one black and one white hat, also a fur cap. He is the property of Capt. James McDonald, of this town. Whoever will bring him to Messrs. McLEAN and BOGLE, shall have the above Reward. All Masters of vessels or others, are hereby warned not to harbour or carry him off, at their peril.

MacDonald, John
Chedabucto, 1784
Enslaved one female, Ruth Vasey.
*Whitfield, p. 229*

MacDonald (Lieut.)
Halifax, 1783
Enslaved one female, Amelia Hopewell, age 21.
*Whitfield, p. 88*
*Book of Negroes*

Mack, Samuel
Annapolis County, 1781
Enslaved one female, Chance, age unknown.
Chance successfully ran away from Mack.
*Harris, Negro Population, p. 18*

MacKinnon, Ranald
Argyle, Yarmouth County, 1760s-1783
Enslaved two people, March and another, name unknown.
*Whitfield, pp. 118, 208*
*Robart-Johnson, p. 37*

Mahan, Timothy
Shelburne, 1791
Enslaved one child, John Simmons, age 5.
*Whitfield, p. 172*

Mallory, Caleb
Granville Township, 1783
Enslaved one male, Joe, age 27.
*Whitfield, p. 104*
*Book of Negroes*

Mallow, Henry (Dr.)
Shelburne, 1783
Enslaved one female, Mary, age unknown.
*Whitfield, p. 123*

Managham, William
Shelburne, 1788
Enslaved at least one person, Mary Postell/Postill, whom he purchased from Jesse Gray for 100 bushels of potatoes. *See Gray, Jesse.*
*Smith, p. 54*

Marshall, Joseph (Captain)
Country Harbour, 1784
Enslaved seven people; Only two known names: Charlotte and Sue.
*Whitfield, pp. 42, 176*
*Smith, p. 26*

Marshall, Elias
Halifax, 1779
Enslaved one woman, Elizabeth Reed/Read.
Elizabeth testified on behalf of Elizabeth Watson (aka Phillis) who unsuccessfully challenged her "Slave" status. Elizabeth testified that she knew Watson as a 'free woman' in the Watson vs. Woodin case.
*Whitfield, p. 158*

Marshall, John
Port Roseway, 1783
Enslaved two people, Plato (age 20) and Richard (40). Both described as 'stout'.
*Hodges, Book Two, p. 148*

Martin's Inn
also known as Martin's Hotel, Mason's Arms, the Trefry Inn, Kempt Lodge, and the old Gilbert Stuart Estate
Newport Corner, 1822
Enslaved at least two males.

*Figure 40: Martin's Inn, Newport Corner, Hants County*
Text on the image reads, at the top "side view" and, at

the bottom, "Martin's Hotel, at Newport Corner, Hants County, when nearing the century mark."

"Tired horses were led away to be fed, watered, groomed and bedded by the African slaves employed there as stablemen... The owners of the Inn in 1822 have not yet been discovered. The building was torn down in 1917."

*Mosher, Old Time Travel, p. 16*

"Mr. James A. Ross, writer and researcher of 'The Story of Newport Township', writes '....the slave bunks on the old (Gilbert) Stuart estate...,coloured slaves slept in the bunks now used as potato bins, on what is known as 'Kempt' Lodge near Newport Corner."

*States, p. 38*

Martin, Jean
Île Royale, 1739
Enslaved one female, Jeanneton, who died at the age of 14.
*Whitfield, p. 101*
*Donovan, "Nominal", pp. 13-14*

Martissans, Pierre
Île Royale, 1741
Enslaved one male, Jean Baptiste (age 15), and Jeanneton (14). Jeanneton was described as a "creole of St. Dominigue" and died at the age of 14. (This is a different woman from the Jeanneton in the previous entry.)
*Whitfield, p. 101*
*Donovan, Slaves and their Owners, pp. 13-14*

Marvin, Joseph
Chester, 1783
Enslaved one male, Jean, age 15.
*Whitfield, p. 101*
*Book of Negroes*

Masonic Lodge (Sydney Branch)
Île Royale, 1791
Enslaved one male, name and age unknown.
*Smith, "The Slave in Canada", pp. 34, 75*

Mauger, Joshua
Halifax & Louisbourg, 1750s
Enslaved and sold people.

Mauger's Beach on McNab's Island in Halifax harbour is named after Joshua Mauger

> "Halifax merchant Joshua Mauger, who traded with Louisbourg throughout the 1750s, 'owned three vessels, manned by his own slaves, captains and crews all Black.'"
>
> *Donovan, Slaves in Île Royale, p. 9*

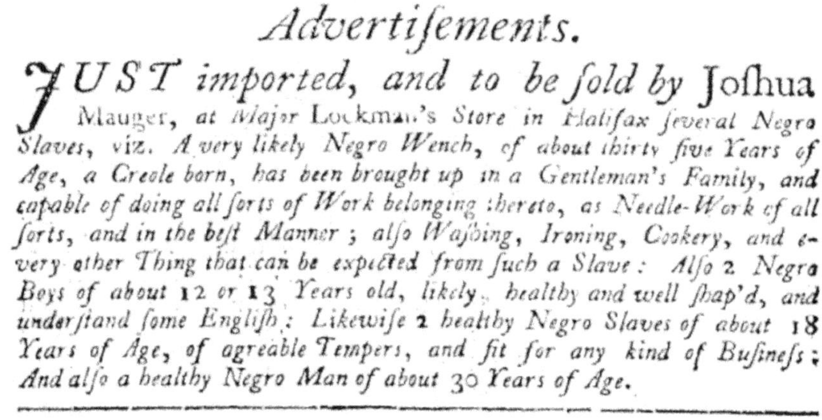

*Advertisements.*

JUST imported, and to be sold by Joshua Mauger, at Major Lockman's Store in Halifax several Negro Slaves, viz. A very likely Negro Wench, of about thirty five Years of Age, a Creole born, has been brought up in a Gentleman's Family, and capable of doing all sorts of Work belonging thereto, as Needle-Work of all sorts, and in the best Manner ; also Washing, Ironing, Cookery, and every other Thing that can be expected from such a Slave : Also 2 Negro Boys of about 12 or 13 Years old, likely, healthy and well shap'd, and understand some English : Likewise 2 healthy Negro Slaves of about 18 Years of Age, of agreable Tempers, and fit for any kind of Business : And also a healthy Negro Man of about 30 Years of Age.

*Figure 41: Slave sale ad by Joshua Mauger, 30 May, 1752*
*Nova Scotia Archives Halifax Gazette 30 May 1752 page 2 (microfilm 8152)*

Maurin, S.
Île Royale, 1752
Enslaved one male, name and age unknown.
*Donovan, "Nominal List of Slaves", p. 158*

McCall, George
Cornwallis, Kings County, 1783
Enslaved one female, Peg, age 16.
*Whitfield, p. 141*
*Book of Negroes*

McCullouch, Alexander (Colonel)
Falmouth, 1763
Enslaved at least two males, names and ages unknown.

> "Colonel Alexander McCulloch, another Planter settler of Falmouth, was also a proprietor of slaves. His so-called 'Negro Servants' are mentioned in the Proceedings of the Court of General Sessions of the Peace of Kings County of 1763 in two cases. In the first case he was charged with assault by Edward Yorke. In the second case he was charged with assault against Abel Michener. In both cases McCulloch had threatened to use his 'Negro servants' to assist in the assaults."
>
> *States, "Presence", p. 36*

McFervey, Nathaniel
Île Royale, 1758
Enslaved one male, Prince Hughine, age unknown.
*Donovan, "Nominal List of Slaves", p. 160*

McInnes (family)
Musquodoboit, 1780s
Enslaved one person of unknown name, age or gender.
*Smith, "The Slave in Canada", p.25*

McKethan, first name unknown
Country Harbour, 1784
Enslaved one male, David, age unknown.
*Whitfield, p. 54*

McAlpine, first name unknown
Shelburne, 1783
Enslaved one child, Jim, age 10.
*Whitfield, p. 102*

McCulloch, first name unknown
Hants County, 1763
Enslaved two people, details unknown.
*States, "Presence and Perseverance", p. 36*

McHeffey, Richard
Windsor, 1791
Enslaved one woman, Clo. Age unknown.

> "Willed to his son, Joseph McHeffey, 'my negro wench called
> Clo', after the death of my said wife, with whom I will and
> direct that my said Negro Girl shall reside and serve, during
> the natural life of my said wife.'"
>
> *States, p. 38*

McIntyre, (Doctor)
Nova Scotia, 1783
Enslaved one child, Prince, age 11.
*Whitfield p. 152*

McKown, John B.
Annapolis Royal
1783
Enslaved one female, Violett, (11)
*Hodges p. 45*

McNeil (also spelled MacNeil and McNeill), Daniel (Captain)
Country Harbour, 1784
Enslaved 'several' people. Only names known are Aggy, Dinnah
(aka Diana) and Fibby
*Whitfield, pp. 12, 58, 110, 116, 159, 161, 170*

McNeill, Daniel
Walton, Hants County
1783
Enslaved an unknown number of people.

> "....Daniel McNeill, a Loyalist from North Carolina, a settler
> on a grant of 1000 acres on the Minas Basin area near
> Walton, Hants County, 'may have brought slaves with him to
> Nova Scotia but tradition says they ran away after being
> told they were free in Nova Scotia.'"
>
> *States, quoting Nellie Fox, p. 45*

McDougall, (Ensign)
Country Harbour, 1784
Enslaved one male, Jeremiah Downan.
*Whitfield, p. 63*

Meek, William
Rawdon, 1792
Enslaved two males, Abraham and Smart.
*Mentioned in the Census of 1792*
*States, p. 45*

Melanson, Baloney
Annapolis/Digby, 1807
Enslaved one female and one child, names unknown.
*Petition of John Taylor and Other Slaveowners*

Melanson, Samuel
Annapolis/Digby, 1807
Enslaved one female and one child, names unknown.
*Petition of John Taylor and Other Slaveowners*

Merserve, Nathaniel
Île Royale, 1746
Enslaved two people, names unknown
*Donovan, Nominal List, p. 160*

Messenger, Ebenezer
Annapolis County, 1771
Enslaved one male, name and age unknown
*Smith, p. 15*

Meyracq, Laurent
Louisbourg, 1745
Enslaved one female, Louise Lawrence.
*Whitfield, p. 112*

Michener, Abel
Hants County, 1794
Enslaved "several"; only known names are Charlot (sic) and James.

The Micheners kept their slaves to the very last, only manumitting them when they were forced to by the government in 1834.
*Blacks in Hants County, p. 36*
*Whitfield pp. 43, 96*

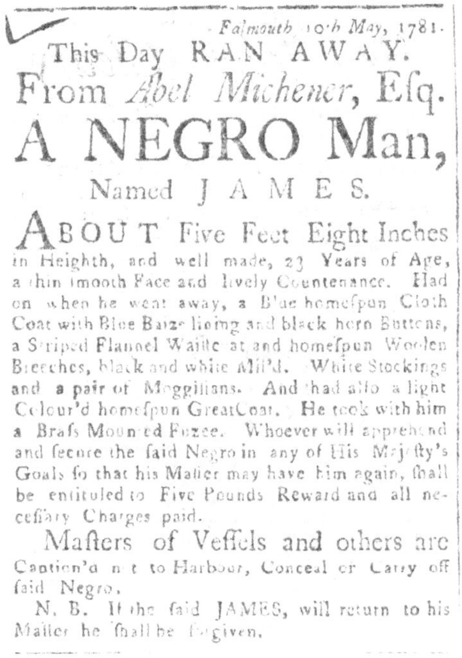

*Falmouth 10th May, 1781.*

This Day RAN AWAY.
From *Abel Michener*, Eſq.
A NEGRO Man,
Named JAMES.

ABOUT Five Feet Eight Inches in Heighth, and well made, 23 Years of Age, a thin ſmooth Face and lively Countenance. Had on when he went away, a Blue homeſpun Cloth Coat with Blue Baize lining and black horn Buttons, a Striped Flannel Waiſtcoat and homeſpun Woolen Breeches, black and white Mill'd. White Stockings and a pair of Moggilians. And had alſo a light Colour'd homeſpun GreatCoat. He took with him a Braſs Mounted Fuzee. Whoever will apprehend and ſecure the ſaid Negro in any of His Majeſty's Goals ſo that his Maſter may have him again, ſhall be entituled to Five Pounds Reward and all neceſſary Charges paid.

Maſters of Veſſels and others are Caution'd not to Harbour, Conceal or Carry off ſaid Negro.

N. B. If the ſaid JAMES, will return to his Maſter he ſhall be forgiven.

*Figure 42: Runaway slave ad from Abel Michener*

*Nova Scotia Gazette May 22, 1781*

*See next page.*

*Figure 43: The Abel Michener House in Mount Denison*
...possibly built in 1765, where Michener's enslaved people worked.
*A.E. Cornwall Nova Scotia Archives 1984-497 number 81 / negative: N-2215*

"Cordelia Patterson, in her compilation of Mount Denson history entitled 'Local History of Mount Denson', asserts that 'the Micheners kept their slaves until the abolition of slavery in 1834.' "

*States, p. 36*

Millidge (Major)
Annapolis Royal, 1783
Enslaved one person, Lydia (20).
*Hodges, Book Two, p. 145*

Mills, (Captain)
Chedabucto, 1783
Enslaved one male, Jack (age 14) and two females, Keziah (20) and Rose (14).
*Whitfield, pp. 91, 111, 162*

Miller, Moses
Truro, 1783
Enslaved one female, Mima (age 26) and Joe (12).
*Whitfield, p. 128*

Milou/Millou, Simone
Île Royale, 1743
Enslaved one female, name and age unknown. She was purchased from Millou as a wife for the Executioner François.
*See Bigot, Francis.*
*Donovan, "Nominal", p. 155*
*Donovan, Slaves in Île Royale, p. 19*

Monis, (Mr.)
Louisbourg, 1745
Enslaved one male, Cuffee, age unknown.
*Whitfield, p. 53*

Montagu/Montague, Charles
Halifax, 1784
Enslaved one male, Francis, age unknown

> "I have only one Negro, named Francis. He is to have his freedom."
>
> *Smith, The Slave in Canada, p. 91*

Moody, James
Annapolis County, 1807
Enslaved eight people, including Bristol and Silvia.
*Petition of John Taylor and Other Slaveowners*

Moody, Margaret
Digby Township, 1807
Enslaved a number of people, names unknown.
*Petition of John Taylor and Other Slaveowners*

Moore (family of)
Parrsboro, dates unknown
Unknown how many people they enslaved.
*Whitfield, p. 222*

Moore, John
Granville township, 1783
Enslaved one male, Joseph, age 30.
*Whitfield, p. 107*
*Book of Negroes*

Moore, Samuel (Captain)
Louisbourg, 1745
Enslaved one male, Gambo, age unknown.
*Donovan, "Nominal List", p. 156*

Moncrief, (Lieutenant Colonel)
Nova Scotia, 1783
Enslaved one male, Emmanuel, age 20.
*Whitfield, p. 65*
*Book of Negroes*

Morel, Jean Baptiste
Île Royale, 1728
Enslaved one male child, Jean Baptiste, age 10.
*Whitfield, p. 101*
*Donovan, "Nominal List", p 152*

Morin, Jean Baptiste and Marie Charlotte Saint Martin
Louisbourg, 1754
Enslaved one male, Hector and one female, Victoire.

Hector and Victoire were the only enslaved couple in Louisbourg permitted to marry. The marriage did not last long, however, as 17-year-old Victoire died five weeks after her wedding.
*Whitfield, p. 80*
*Donovan, "Slaves in Île Royale", pp. 30-31*

Morpain, Pierre
Louisbourg, 1732
*Enslaved one male, George, aka Sauzy.*
*Donovan, "Slaves and Their Owners", pp. 25-26*

> Donovan writes:
> "Louisbourg port captain Pierre Morpain had his seven year old slave Georges Sauzy baptized on 17 June 1732....As port captain, Morpain was one of the key defenders of Louisbourg during the siege of 1745, leading a detachment of 80 men to Bagarus Bay to prevent a landing by the New Englanders...Although wounded during the fray, Morpain was saved by his slave. According to Antoine de la Boularderie, co-leader of the expedition, 'his negro carried him, dragged him, hid him under some leaves and saved him. In recognition of his services, he gave him his liberty and they only returned to the town three days later under great personal risk.'...Sauzy, only 24 years old, returned to Louisbourg and settled on the Mira River, a free man."

Morris, Christopher
Halifax, 1783
Enslaved two people: one female, Amoretta (age unknown) and Solomon (12) described as 'a fine boy'.
*Book of Negroes*
*Hodges, p. 48*

Morris, Charles III - Surveyor General of Nova Scotia
Halifax, 1783
Enslaved one male child, Solomon, age 12.
*Whitfield, p. 175*

The Morris family were surveyors in the early settler era of Nova Scotia. This is the grandson of the first Charles Morris, who surveyed many of the interior roads and the African Nova Scotian settlements and land grants in Nova Scotia.

Morris Street in Halifax is named for Charles Morris III, as his offices were located there.

Morris, James
July 26, 1806
Enslaved one man, Prince, to take with him to Sable Island.

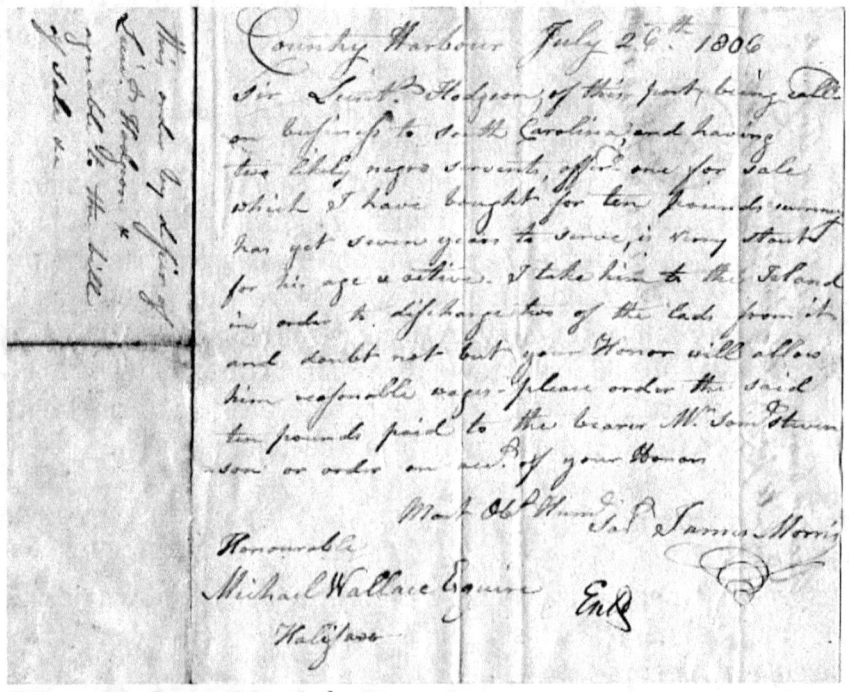

*Figure 44: James Morris letter*
...to Michael Wallace of Country Harbour.
    *Nova Scotia Archives RG 31 series 120 volume 2 number 160*

> "James Morris writes to inform of his purchase of a 'likely negro servant' from Sir Lieutenant Hodgson, who has been called on business to South Carolina. Morris intends for this servant to be put to work on Sable Island for 'reasonable wages'."

Enslaved peoples' work was often contracted out with the Enslaver/Owner receiving the monies the enslaved person earned for them.

*See Wallace, James for his response to Morris.*

Murray, Margaret
Halifax, 1787
Enslaved two females, Marianne and Flora and one child, Brutus.
*Whitfield p. 31*

> "I do manumit my two Negro women, Marianne and Flora, and also my Negro boy Brutus when he shall arrive at the age of twenty-one years."
> *Smith, p. 91-92*

# N

Nash, John
Chedabucto, 1783
Enslaved four people; Bina and her son Pompey; Charles and Cyrus.
*Whitfield, p. 2*

Noble, Jesse
Nova Scotia , 1785
Enslaved one man, John Gibson aka John Boocher.
*Whitfield, p. 75*

Norris, John
Nova Scotia, 1783
Enslaved one female, Elizabeth (24) and Jacob (age unknown).
*Book of Negroes*
*Whitfield, pp. 65, 95*

Northup, Jeremiah
Falmouth, 1798
Enslaved one male, James Grant, age unknown. James attempted to run away from Northup.
*Whitfield, p. 76*

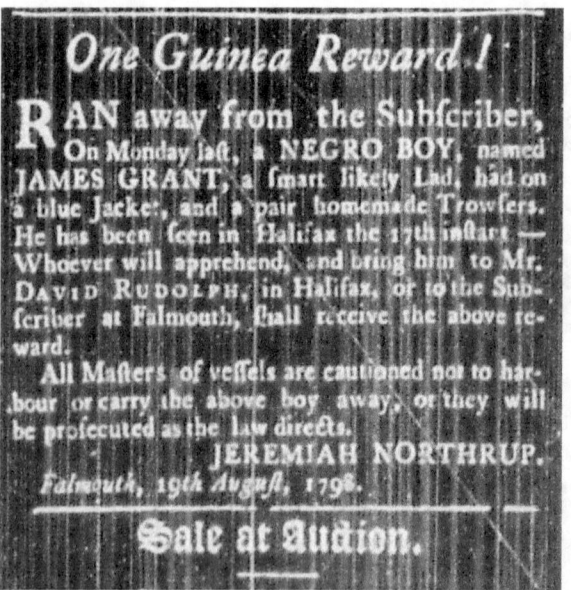

*Figure 45: Jeremiah Northrup runaway slave ad*

...in the *Royal Gazette* of October 24, 1780 to any person who would bring his "negro boy named James Grant, a smart, likely lad" to Mr. David Rudolph of Halifax or to himself at Falmouth.

*Smith, p. 62*

Northup, Joseph
Halifax, 1779
Enslaved one male, Mintur. Northup sold Mintur to John Palmer of Falmouth for £100. Mintur eventually got his freedom and named his firstborn son Freeman.
*Whitfield, p. 128*

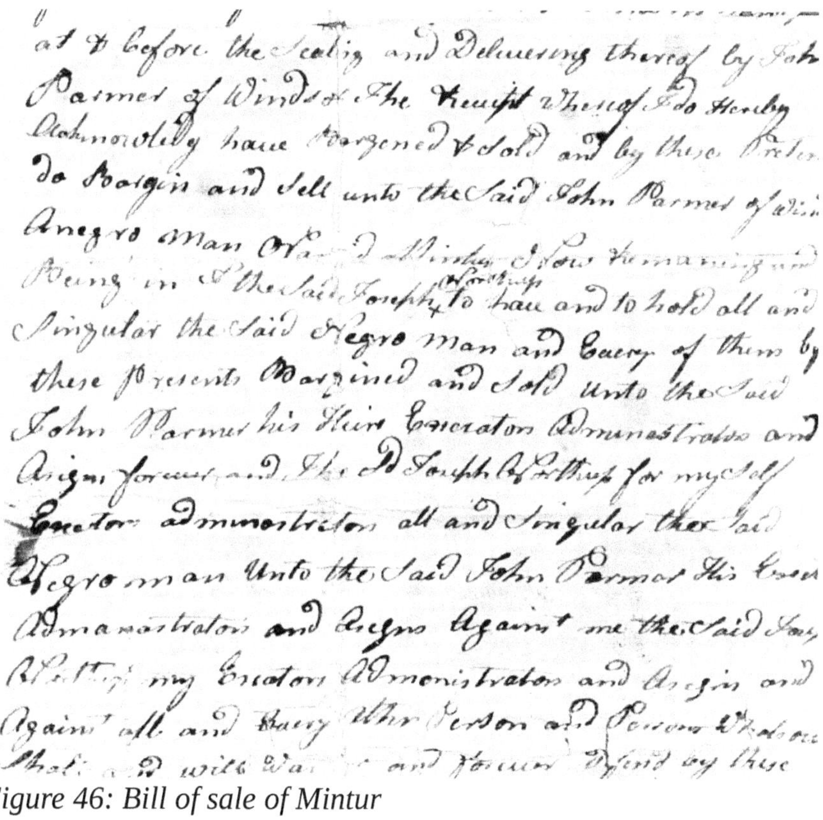

*Figure 46: Bill of sale of Mintur*
...,African Nova Scotian Enslaved man, from Joseph Northup to John Palmer of Windsor for the sum of One Hundred Pounds.

*https://archives.novascotia.ca/africanns/archives/?ID=1*

Nutter, Valentine
Shelburne, 1783
Enslaved one female, Silvia (age 30), and one male Sam (age 22).
*Whitfield, pp. 165, 171*

# O

Oakes, Jesse
Bridgetown, dates unknown
Enslaved two men, Black Cato and Black James.
*Harris, p. 16*

O'Dell, Daniel (and Earl, Philip)
Annapolis Royal, 1783
Enslaved one male, Joe, who ran away from him.
*Whitfield, p. 139*

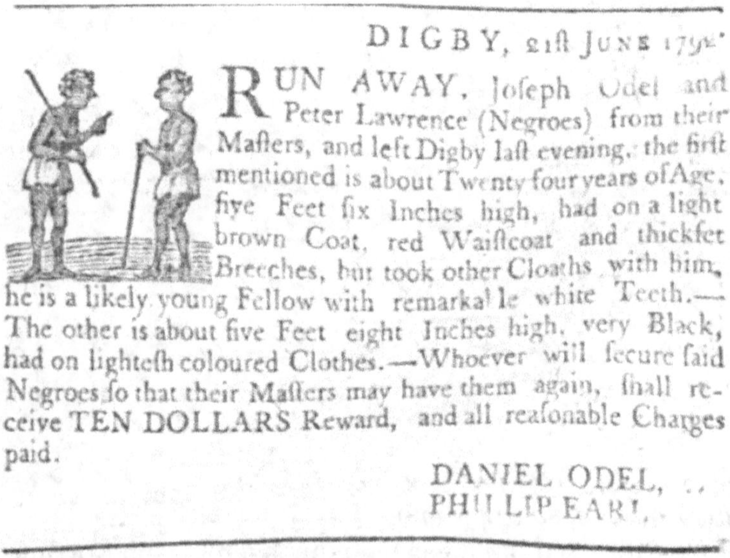

DIGBY, 21ft June 1792.

RUN AWAY, Jofeph Odel and Peter Lawrence (Negroes) from their Mafters, and left Digby laft evening, the firft mentioned is about Twenty four years of Age, five Feet fix Inches high, had on a light brown Coat, red Waiftcoat and thickfet Breeches, but took other Cloaths with him, he is a likely young Fellow with remarkable white Teeth.— The other is about five Feet eight Inches high, very Black, had on lightefh coloured Clothes.—Whoever will fecure faid Negroes fo that their Mafters may have them again, fhall receive TEN DOLLARS Reward, and all reafonable Charges paid.

DANIEL ODEL,
PHILLIP EARL.

*Figure 47: Runaway ad for Joseph Odel and Peter Lawrence
...placed in The Royal Gazette July 3, 1792 by their 'masters'*

Daniel Odel (O'Dell) and Phillip Earl.

# P

Palmer, John
Halifax
1779
Enslaved one man, Mintaur, whom he purchased from Joseph
Northup of Falmouth. Palmer is recorded as having other enslaved
people.
*Whitfield, p. 128*
*States, p. 36*
*See Northup, Joseph for the bill of sale.*

> "L.S. Loomer (Windsor, Nova Scotia: a journey in History,
> 1996) states that "the Palmers owned other slaves whose
> names are not remembered. There is a Palmer family tradi-
> tion that every night Mintur disappeared until it was dis-
> covered he was going up river to hew out a boat to take him
> back to what became the United States. On one occasion he
> was discovered on his way to the river, hauling the boat be-
> hind him."
>
> *States, p. 37*

Paris, M
Île Royale, 1756
Enslaved one female, unknown name and age.
*Whitfield, p. 224*

Parker, (Captain)
Île Royale, 1760
Enslaved one man, unknown name and age
*Donovan, Nominal List, p. 160*

Parker, (Mrs.)
Liverpool, 1790
Enslaved one male, Ned, age unknown.
*Whitfield, p. 137*
*Diary of Simeon Perkins, p. 29*

Parker, Peter
Shelburne, 1791
Enslaved one male, Isaac Luther, age unknown.
*Whitfield, p. 117*
*Royal Gazette July 12, 1791*

Parkin, (Mr.)
Shelburne, 1783
Enslaved one female, Violet, and her child Dick Parkin (6 mos.).
Possibly fathered by Parkin.
*Whitfield, p. 140*
*Book of Negroes*

Pascault, M.
Île Royale, 1753
Enslaved one male, Polidor.
*Donovan, "Slaves and their owners", p. 158*

Patten (family of)
Parrsboro, dates unknown
Enslaved an unknown number of people.
*Whitfield, p. 222*

Patton, John
Malagash, 1783
Enslaved one female, Hannah, age unknown.
*Whitfield, p. 78*
*Book of Negroes*

Patton, Nathaniel
Île Royale, 1760
Enslaved one male, Rumford. age unknown.
*Whitfield, p. 164*

Pearson, Moses
Louisbourg, 1787
Enslaved one male, Cuffee Hominey/Hominy. Age Unknown
*Whitfield p. 86*

Pepperell, William
Ile Royale
1745
Enslaved one male, Cato, age unknown.
*Donovan, "Slaves and their owners", p. 24*

Pere, John
Île Royale, 1743
Enslaved one female, Marie, and her three children: Madeleine,
Marie and Victor.
*Whitfield, p. 120*
*Donovan, "Female Sexual Slaves", pp. 153-156*

Peres, Marie Anne
Louisbourg, 1735
Enslaved one male, Georges Peres, age unknown.
*Donovan, Slaves and their Owners, p. 27*

*See next page*

*Figure 48: The Peres home in Louisbourg, 1735*
George Peres would have lived on the fish shack to the far right
of this sketch.

   *Image courtesy of Ken Donovan Slaves and Their Owners, p. 27*

Perkins, Simeon
Liverpool, 1777
Enslaved one male, Jacob (aka Frank), age unknown.
*Whitfield, p. 95*

*Figure 49: Simeon Perkins house, Liverpool*
This is now a museum. Think of Jacob when you visit it.

   *archives.novascotia.ca/builtheritage/archives/?ID=64*

Peters, Samuel
Halifax, 1783
Enslaved one male, Harry, age 12.
*Whitfield, p. 81*

Phillips, (Captain)
Halifax, 1783
Enslaved one male, George, age 13.
*Whitfield, p. 73*

Philips, Captain
Annapolis Royal, 1783
Enslaved one male, Anthony Philips, age 23.
*Hodges, p. 44*

Pierpont, Joseph
Halifax, 1773
Enslaved one male, Prince.
*Smith, "Slaves", p. 10*

Pithou, first name unknown
Île Royale, 1724
Enslaved two people, unknown names and ages.
*Donovan "Nominal List" p. 152*

Plummer, Enoch (69th Regiment of Foot)
Halifax, 1783
Enslaved one female, Rose, and her four-month-old child, James,
possibly fathered by Plummer.
*Whitfield, p. 162*

Polhemus, John
Clementsport, 1807
Enslaved ten people: Edward, George, Marshal, Mary, Joseph,
Caesar, Slyvia, Samuel, Rose, Unknown. Ages unknown.
*Petition of John Taylor and Other Slaveowners*
*Whitfield, pp.64, 122, 124, 162*

### Built by Slaves
*Interesting Historical Sketch of the Recently Burned Potter
House*

More about the history, as told to me, of the James D Potter
house, which was recently destroyed by fire, might interest
some of the older generation.

The original owner, Miss Mary Polhemus, being a United
Empire Loyalist was given a large grant of land in the township of Clements with boundaries running along the old
post road, now known as the Back Road, north and south to
the Guinea Road, thence along the Guinea road to Moose
River Brook, thence along the brook where the old race way
used to be for the flour mills, thence north and south to the
shore of Annapolis Basin. The land then being covered by
heavy timber, she soon had her slaves whom she brought
with her cutting trees and had them hewed where they fell,
and built 3 barns and the hold house. Also, to the west end
of the old house, there was a building for storing rum for
the slaves; the old ship that was on the east end of the
present house was the slaves' quarters. Some of them still
remained with their owners after being liberated.

It seems Miss Polhemus was very particular about the
appearance of her horses and when injections[??]. A few
days ago I [??] was starting out for her drive about the
place, she had a white silk handkerchief to wipe them
down; if it showed any dirt the slaves had to groom the
horses all over again, and the coachman was called to halt,

to pick up any goose feathers scattered about the road. However, there came a time when 2 nephews came to visit her, they being her heirs. These mischievous lads put a lizard in her tea kettle and she brewed some tea, but after drinking it left her in a state of paralysis the rest of her life. The 2 nephews finally died in a prison in the State of New Jersey.

Miss Polhemus's last resting place was in the old St Edward's Cemetery at Clementsport. James D Potter and his brother, Robert, purchased the land from her relative and executor, Jeremiah Vanderbilt of New Jersey in 1850, remaining in their possession until their death, Dec 24th, 1910, when the son-in-law, Charles Essensa, had possession until 1919, then the present owner, Arthur Essenza.

*Annapolis Royal Spectator, March 25, 1937*
*\*Special thank you to Wilfred Allan for*
*bringing this article to my attention.*

Porter, John
Cornwallis, 1784
Enslaved one male, unknown name and age.
*Smith, The Slave in Canada, p. 17*

Potts, (family)
Parrsboro, dates unknown
Enslaved an unknown number of people; no details available.
*Whitfield, p. 222*

Potts, (Mr.)
Shelburne, 1783
Enslaved one child, Jenny Bolton, age 11.
*Book of Negroes*
*Whitfield, p. 29*

Potts, (Mr.)
Port Roseway, 1783
Enslaved one female, Jenny Bolton (11).
*Hodges, Book Two, p. 145*

Prévost, Jacques
Île Royale, 1749
Enslaved four people: Angelique and her child Jacques, Jean Narcisse, Pierre.
*Donovan, "Slaves and their Owners", p. 11*

Prince, David
Liverpool, 1777
Enslaved one male, name unknown
*Diary of Simeon Perkins 1766-1780, p. 166*

Pringle, Elizabeth Susanna
Halifax, 1781
Enslaved one man, Cato, whom she inherited from her father, Richard Wenman.
Pringle was supposed to have Cato for two years and then he was to be manumitted.
*Smith, p. 91*

Pritchard, Martha
Digby/Annapolis counties, 1777
Enslaved one female, Jesse, and her child, John Patten, age 2.
*Whitfield, p. 103*
*Book of Negroes*

Proctor, Charles
Halifax, 1767
Enslaved one person, Louisa, whom he sold in Bridgetown to Mrs. Reverend Mary Day who, in turn, "assigned over" Louisa to her daughter, Mrs. Mary Day.
*Smith, pp. 15-16*

Proud, William
Halifax, 1778
Enslaved one female, Elizabeth Watson Reed (aka Phillis).
*Whitfield, p. 158*

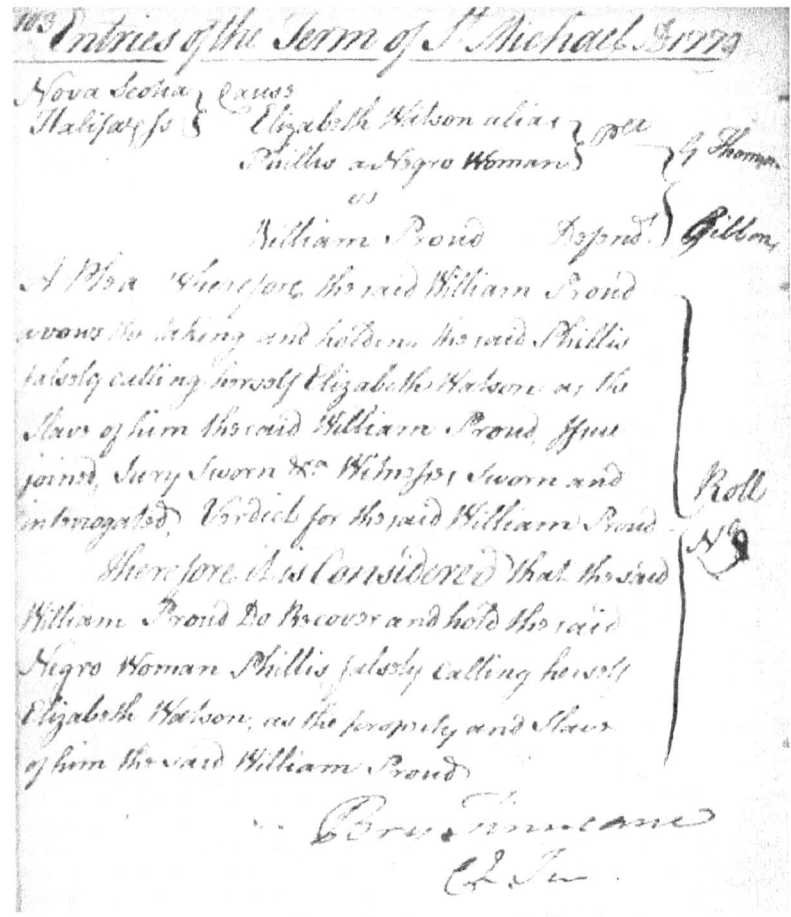

*Figure 50: Document from the lawsuit of Elizabeth Watson*

...(aka Phillis) versus William Proud. Watson was brought to Nova Scotia from Boston, where she was a free woman. In Nova Scotia she was bought by Proud, a butcher, who abused her. Watson sued for unlawful confinement and £100 in damages. Proud's witness was Samuel Laha, who said he owned

Watson in Boston. Watson lost her case and was returned to Proud.

*Supreme Court of Nova Scotia, 1779 - Halifax County*
*Judgement books, Nova Scotia Archives*
*RG 39 J Halifax County Vol. 6, p.103*

Purdy, Bethiah
Annapolis Royal/Clements township, 1807
Enslaved an unknown number of people.
*Petition of John Taylor and Other Slaveowners*

Purdy, Elijah
Annapolis Royal/Clements township, 1807
Enslaved one male and two females. All unknown names and ages.
*Petition of John Taylor and Other Slaveowners*

Purdy, Gabriel
Clements township, 1783
Enslaved seven people, including Ned Moore, Belinda, Hester, Ned Moore Jr., Peter and Sue (age 21).
*Whitfield, pp. 129, 142*

Purdy/Purdie, Gabriel
Cobequid, 1783
Enslaved one female, Lydia, age 15.
*Whitfield pp. 129, 142, 176*
*Hodges, p. 56*

Purdy, Henry (Colonel)
Amherst - Fort Lawrence, unknown dates
Enslaved one female, Slyvey.
*Whitfield, p. 155*

# R

Randall, David
Wilmot, 1785
Enslaved one female, Sukey. age unknown.
*Perkins, p. 137*
*Whitfield, p. 178*

> "Item, I give Kezia, my said wife, a red milch cow without horns and my black mare, and also the use of my negro wench, Sukey, during the life of my said wife and after the death of my wife, I give my said negro wench to my said daughter Newcome and granddaughter Mary Shay to be by them sold, and the money arriving from the sale to be equally divided between them, share and share alike."
> *Will of David Randall, 1785, Annapolis County, NS Archives*

Ratchford, (family)
Partridge Island, dates unknown
Enslaved an unknown number of people.
*Whitfield, p. 222*

Raymond (family)
Parrsboro, unknown years
Enslaved an unknown number of people.
*Whitfield, p. 222*

Read, Isaac
Port Roseway, 1783
Enslaved four people:  John Warren (age 45), Basan Vaughan (25), Leah (4) and Lilly (30).
*Hodges, Book Two, p. 148*

Reed, Stephen
Amherst, 1801
Enslaved two people, names unknown.
*Smith, The Slave in Canada, p. 84*

> "...requests his sons 'jointly to provide for and comfortably take care of the black man and black woman slaves belonging to me, during their natural lives.'"
> *Will of Stephen Reed, 1801, Cumberland County NS Archives*

Reynolds, Andrew
Nova Scotia, 1790
Enslaved one male, Dick.
*Whitfield, p. 60*

Rhodes, Samuel
Louisbourg, 1745
Enslaved one male, unknown name, described as "Negro Drummer".
*Whitfield, p. 137*
*Donovan "Nominal", p. 156*

Richardson, (Mrs.)
Halifax, 1780
Enslaved two males, Ben Porter and Silas Ruen (age 18).
*Whitfield, p 149*

Rinn, Mary
Shelburne, 1783
Enslaved eight people: Fanny (age 22), Anthony Jones (4), Bill (40), Carsy (28), Charles (22), Sentry (28) and their child, and Phillis (32).
*Whitfield pp. 68, 106, 160, 169*

Robertson, William
Horton Township, 1804
Enslaved one female child, Percilla, age 8 years.
The last slave sold in NS.
*Acadian University Archives Collection of Arthur Wentworth Hamilton Eaton*

Robie, Hannah Lee & Bradstreet, Mary
Halifax, 1780s
Both women enslaved one female, Flora and her son, Prince. Robie originally owned them, and when she passed, Bradstreet inherited them.
*Whitfield, p. 70*

Robins, Joseph
Shelburne, 1786
Enslaved two males, Pero and Tom. Ages unknown.
*Whitfield, p. 141*
*General Sessions at Shelburne MG4, vol. 141, NSA*

"The other 1786 case involved men named Pero and Tom. Joseph Robins claimed that he had purchased both men for £29 sterling...During his examination, Pero stated that he had gone to St. Augustine with James Stone, instead of returning to his rebel master. But he denied being the property of Stone. Tom, for his part, commented that he had belonged to Philip Caine in "Carolina" and had run away to Charleston, where he worked in the wood yard. Tom accompanied Joseph Robins to St. Augustine...The court ordered Joseph Robins to "take Possession" of Tom and Pero, but required that he not sell them out of the province for 12 months. The continued enslavement or re-enslavement of blacks is instructive for several reasons. Tom and Pero both realised that they could assert their freedom in court. Although they lost, they either told the truth or were smart enough to construct a narrative that aligned with the history of most free blacks in the region—that is, running away from a rebel owner and performing loyal services to His Majesty before migrating to St. Augustine and finally Nova Scotia. These slaves realized that the legalities of slavery and freedom were shifting and unclear. They attempted to use the confusion to gain their freedom."

*Whitfield, "The Struggle", page 35*

Robinson, Beverley
Wilmot, 1784
Enslaved seven people, ages ten and up and two people under the age of ten, all names unknown.
*Harris, p. 6*

Robinson, Robert
Granville Township, 1800
Enslaved one boy, name and age unknown
*Whitfield, p. 192*

Robinson, Wilbur
Annapolis Royal, 1804
Bought one female, Pricilla, from the estate of Robert Dickson.

"A conveyance was found not so many years ago in the cellar of the late Peter Bonnett, once High Sheriff of the County, dated 1804, from Isaac Bonnett and other administrators of the estate of Robert Dickson, late of Annapolis to Wilbur Robinson and his heirs & of 'a certain negro girl slave named Pricilla about 6 years and 4 months of age, being part of the personal estate of the late Robert Dickson, and after the usual form guarantees to the purchaser the right to the possession and service of the slave.'"

*Harris, p. 14*

Robinson, Thomas
Shelburne, 1786
Enslaved four people; two males, Manuel and Phillip, one female,
Priscilla and her child Sally.
*Whitfield, pp. 118, 144, 155*

Robblee, Thomas
Granville Township, 1784
Enslaved four people, names unknown.
*Harris, p. 6*

Rock, John
Halifax, 1772
Enslaved at least one person, a girl named Thursday. She ran away
from Rock.

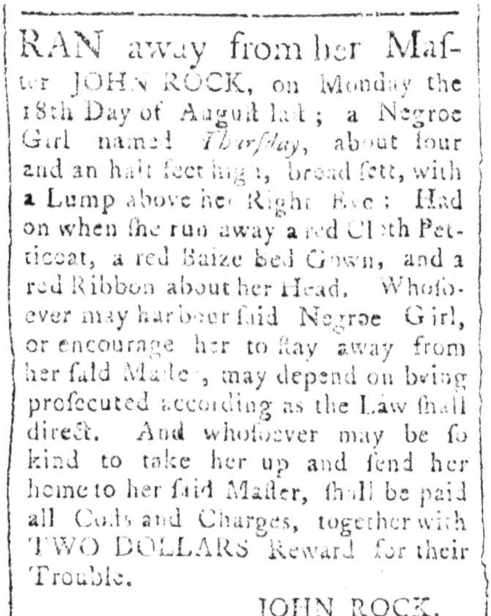

RAN away from her Maf-
ter JOHN ROCK, on Monday the
18th Day of August laſt; a Negroe
Girl named *Thurſday*, about four
and an half feet high, broad fett, with
a Lump above her Right Eye: Had
on when fhe run away a red Cloth Petticoat, a red Baize bed Gown, and a
red Ribbon about her Head. Whoſoever may harbour faid Negroe Girl,
or encourage her to ſtay away from
her faid Maſter, may depend on being
profecuted according as the Law fhall
direct. And whoſoever may be fo
kind to take her up and fend her
home to her faid Maſter, fhall be paid
all Cofts and Charges, together with
TWO DOLLARS Reward for their
Trouble.
                               JOHN ROCK.
HALIFAX, Sept. 1ſt, 1772.

*Figure 51: Advertisement placed by
John Rock*

...about his runaway slave, Thursday, in the *Nova
Scotia Gazette* September 1, 1772.

Rodrigue, Antoine
Île Royale, 1754
Enslaved one female, Marie Clemence.
*Donovan, "Nominal", p. 159*

Rodrigue, M (wife of)
Île Royale, 1733
Enslaved one female, Rose, and one child, Catherine Francoise, age 7.
*Whitfield, p. 37*

Rodrigue, Michel
Île Royale, 1742
Enslaved one male, Laurent.
*Whitfield, p. 112*

Roma, Jean Pierre
Louisbourg, 1748-49
Enslaved 12 people, including Barbe and her daughter Marie, and St. Jean.
*Whitfield, pp. 18, 175*

Ross, Alexandar
Port Roseway, 1783
Enslaved one male, William Robertson, 36.
*Hodges, Book One, p. 44*

Ross, George
Shelburne, 1806-07
Enslaved one female, Catherine Edwards.
*Whitfield p. 64*

Rowland, John (Reverend)
Shelburne, 1798
Enslaved one female, name unknown, and two males, Samuel and
William.
*Whitfield, p. 194*

Ruggles, Richard
Annapolis County , 1783
Enslaved one male, Prince, age unknown.
*Whitfield, p. 152*

Ruggles, Timothy (Brigadier General)
Wilmot/Spa Springs, 1783
Enslaved between five and nine people, including  Hester (age 7),
Jeffery (6), Prince (19), Robert Williams (23) and John Coslin (25
and noted to be Mulatto).
*Donovan, "Slavery and Freedom" introduction*

For more about the Ruggles 'plantation', read "Searching for the
Enslaved in Nova Scotia's Loyalist Landscape" by Catherine M.A.
Cottreau-Robins. journals.lib.unb.ca/index.php/acadiensis/art-
icle/view/22041/25575

Russell, Joseph
Cole Harbour, 1784
Enslaved four people Bristol, Nanny, William and Katty (age 6).
*Whitfield, pp. 30, 110, 135, 232*

Rutherford, Henry
Annapolis Royal/Digby, 1807
Enslaved four people: one female, one male; two children, names
unknown
*uelac.org/PDF/Land-Transfers-From-Slave-Owning-Loyalists-Son-
to-the-African-Baptist-Church-by-Brian-McConnell.pdf*

Ryerson, John
Yarmouth, 1783
Enslaved three people; two females, Priscilla (age 32) and Sarah
(22), and Sam (2)
*Book of Negroes*
*Whitfield, pp. 154, 168*

Ryerson, Peter
Port Roseway, 1784
Enslaved two males, Caesar (sic) and 'a boy 9 years of age'.
*Hodges, p. 7*

# S

Saint Paul's Anglican Church
Halifax, 1801
Enslaved one person, name unknown, inherited from Stephen
Reed of Amherst in his Last Will and Testament.

> "An equally benevolent intention may have prompted the
> slave-owner who either gave or bequeathed a slave for the
> 'use and benefit of the wardens and vestry of St. Paul's, Hal-
> ifax.'
>
> *Smith "The Slave in Canada", p. 85*

*See next page.*

*Figure 52: St. Paul's Anglican Church, Halifax, 1890*
*Notman Studio Nova Scotia Archives*
*accession no. 1983-310 no. 53.2 | neg. no. N-5124*

Salter, Malachy
Halifax, 1759
Enslaved two people, Hagar and Jack.
Salter Street, Halifax is named after him.
*Smith, p. 6*

Salter was a well known businessman and one of the first members of assembly in early Halifax. Salter lived at what is now the corner of Salter and Barrington Streets, Halifax.

*See next page.*

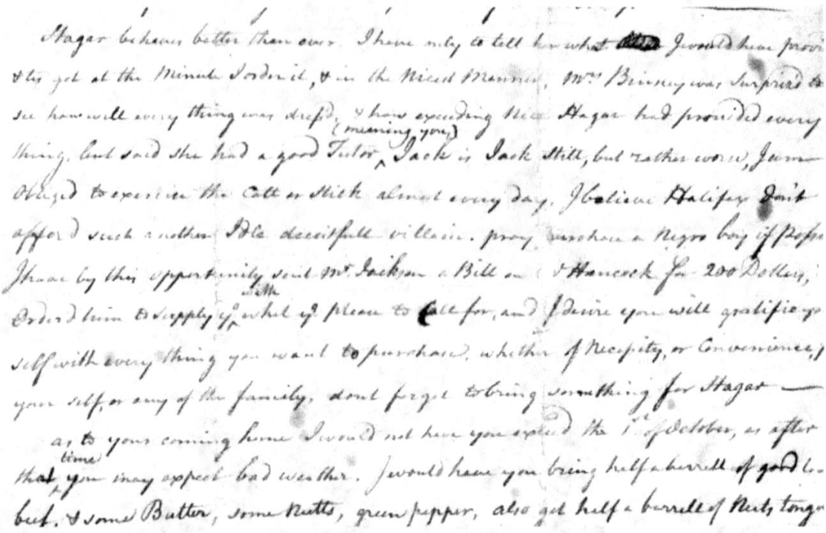

Hagar behaves better than ever. I have only to tell her what I would have provi
& tis got at the Minute I order it, & in the Nicest Manner, Mrs Binney was surprized to
see how well every thing was dress'd, & how exceeding Neat Hagar had provided every
thing, but said she had a good Tutor (meaning you) Jack is Jack Still, but rather worse, I am
Obliged to exercise the Catt or Stick almost every day. I believe Halifax don't
afford such another Idle deceitfull villain. pray purchase a Negro boy if possi
I have by this opportunity sent Mr. Jackson a Bill on & Hancock for 200 Dollars,
Ordered him to supply you with what you please to Call for, and I desire you will gratifie yo
self with every thing you want to purchase, whether of Necessity, or Conveniency,
your self or any of the family, don't forget to bring something for Hagar —
as to your coming home I would not have you exceed the 1st of October, as after
that time you may expect bad weather. I would have you bring half a barrell of good b
beef, & some Butter, some Nutts, green pepper, also get half a barrell of Neats tongu

*Figure 53: Malachy Salter letter to his wife*
...Sept. 2,1759, in which he discusses their slaves Hagar and Jack. Salter complains about Jack, calling him an '..idle deceitful villain' who needs to feel the 'catt or stick almost everyday.'"

*archives.novascotia.ca/pdf/africanns/*
*F90N85-SlaveInCanada.pdf p.6*

Savage, (Mrs.)
Port Roseway, 1783
Enslaved one female, Dinah Archer, age 42. Described as 'stout wench, one eyed'.
*Hodges, Book Two, p. 148*

Scribner, Joseph
Amherst, 1783
Enslaved one male, Isaac, age 17.
*Whitfield, p. 89*
*Book of Negroes*

Scott, Henry
Windsor Township (Eastern District), 1794
Enslaved one man, John, age unknown.
*States, p. 46*

Seabury, David
Annapolis Royal, 1783-84
Enslaved three people, all adults. Will (age 23) and two others.
*Frost and States, Section 2, pp. 30-31*
*Hodges, p. 118*

Seccombe, (Reverend)
Chester, 1760s
Enslaved three people; one female Dinah and two males, John and
Soloman.
One of the founders of Chester.
*Whitfield, pp. 61, 105, 175*
*States, p. 44*

Seigneur, John
Île Royale, 1728
Enslaved two females, Louise (age 25) and Etienne (14).
*Donovan, "Slaves and Their Owners", pp. 20-21*

> "...Panis slave, Louise, who arrived from Quebec during the
> summer of 1727. Louisbourg innkeeper Jean Seigneur pur-
> chased the 25 year old Louise from captain Pierre Dauteuil
> in order to use her as a servant in his inn....By February
> 1728, however, Seigneur realized that Louise was eight or
> nine months pregnant and therefore unsuitable as a servant
> in his establishment. In Louisbourg, as in France, it was cus-
> tomary to discharge servant girls as soon as they became
> pregnant in order to avoid public scandal. Seigneur now re-
> fused to keep Louise, on the grounds that she 'gave a poor
> example to his family, especially his young daughters, and
> because he could not call on her services which he needed

in his inn'. A priest, Michel Leduff, was summoned for a private discussion with Louise and learned that, on the voyage from Quebec during the summer of 1727, when 'the crew were quiet', Louise had slept in Dauteil's cabin and was now expecting his child. Dauteuil had sold her to Seigneur, warning her to say nothing, but promising to return for her prior to the birth of the baby. Since she was a slave, Louise had little choice but to obey Dauteil and no recourse should he fail to keep his promise. Louise delivered baby Louis on 3 April and he was baptized, with Seigneur's daughter Angelique acting as godmother. Four months after the birth, Dauteuil and Seigneur appeared before a Louisbourg notary and agreed that Louise and her baby should be sold in Martinique in favour of another slave. One year later, Louise had been sold in Martinique for 600 livres and replaced by 14 year old Etienne."

*Donovan, "Slaves in Île Royale", pp. 20-21*

Note that Louise is Panis, a term of the time for indigenous North Americans, not African.

Selkring, James
Shelburne, 1784
Enslaved one male, Peter.
*Whitfield, p. 142*

Shakespeare, Stephen
Shelburne, 1783
Enslaved twenty people; names and ages unknown.
*Smith, p. 23*

Shatford, Daniel
Halifax, 1779
Enslaved one male, Adam.
Shatford left Adam to his wife upon his death and, upon her death,
Adam went to their daughter, Sarah Lawson.
*Smith, p. 14*

Sheaffe, Edward
Louisbourg, 1760
Enslaved one boy, Cato Sheaffe.
*Whitfield, p. 170*

Sherman, Jonathan
Cornwallis, 1801-1834
Enslaved three people; one woman, Chloe, and her two sons Isaac
Willioughby and one other.
Isaac made a public complaint about the treatment of his mother.
*Whitfield, pp. 49, 233-234*

Shey, William Henry (Colonel)
Green Grove Farm, Falmouth, 1769 to 1854
Enslaved one person, Juba Caesar.
*States, "Presence and Perseverance"*

> "An article entitled 'Old Time Reminiscences' appeared in a
> 1911 Windsor newspaper and included the following: The
> writer remembers well when Col. Wm. Shey owned and oc-
> cupied the above-mentioned property, together with the
> buildings which were kept in fine shape. Juba Caesar was a
> coloured slave brought here by old Mr. Shey and at his
> death came into possession of Col. Shey. Juba was a faithful
> servant, and when he died Col. Shey had his remains placed
> in the family lot. The writer has often been told by his par-
> ents and grandparents of Juba. He had a gift of relating the
> reminiscences of his life and one special topic was how very
> kind Massa Shey had been to him. One of his presents to

him was a flock of sheep and Juba said 'in dem dar sheeps war big money, and all dat Massa Shey axed for keeping dem dar sheeps was de wool and de lambs'."

*States, "Presence and Perseverance"*

*Figure 54: Gravestone of Juba Caesar*
"Sacred to the Memory of Juba Caesar who departed this life Feby 26th 1845 Aged 76 Years"

*States, "Growing up Black"*

Shey, Peter
Falmouth, 1776
Enslaved one known person, Dinah, after he purchased her from
the Reverend John Breynton of Halifax.
*https://archives.novascotia.ca/africanns/archives/?ID=12*

Sickles, Daniel
Port Roseway, 1783
Enslaved one male, Anthony Jarvis.
*Whitfield, p. 100*
*Book of Negroes*

Simmons, (Mr.)
Liverpool, 1791
Enslaved one male named either David or William.
*Whitfield pp. 55, 233*

Sinclair, Frederick
Annapolis Royal, 1787
Enslaved one female, Jane, age unknown.
*Whitfield, p. 100*
*Harris, "Negro Population", pp 17-18*

> An Historical Event
> The following copy of a document disposing of a negro
> slave in Annapolis, Nova Scotia 115 years ago [therefore in
> 1787], will be interesting to many of our readers. The writ-
> ing is as legible, and the paper is as good a state of preser-
> vation, as though it were one hundred and fifteen weeks, in-
> stead of years old.
> Know all men by these presents that I Richard Betts, of the
> city of New York, for and in consideration of the sum of
> twenty one pounds, current money of the Province of Nova
> Scotia, to me in hand paid at and before the sealing and dis-
> posing of these presents by Frederick Sinclair, of the Town-
> ship of Annapolis, have granted, bargained, and sold; and

now by these presents do grant, bargain and sell unto the said Frederick Sinclair, a negro wench unto the said Frederick Sinclair, his heirs and assigns, against all persons whatever, forever warrant and defend.

In witness whereof I have hereunto set my hand and seal, this 24th day of February, 1787.

RICHARD BETTS

Sealed and delivered in the presence of Christopher Bomon, William Benson.

*Annapolis Spectator, Friday, May 9, 1902*

*Figure 55: The Sinclair Inn, Annapolis Royal*
Today it is a museum. Think of Jane when you visit here.

Snelling, Jonathan
Rawding. 1794-95
Enslaved one male, Jack.
*Whitfield, p. 217*
*Petition of John Taylor*
*States, p. 45*

Snodgrass, Andrew
Annapolis County, 1807
Enslaved one person, unknown gender, name and age.
*Petition of John Taylor*

Sommerville, Robert
Shelburne, 1786
Enslaved one male, Joe.
*Whitfield, p. 105*

Solignac, Francois
Île Royale, 1759
Enslaved one male, unknown name and age.
*Donovan, Nominal List, p. 160*

Spellen, James (Captain)
Île Royale, 1753
Enslaved one male child, Jean (age 11).
*Whitfield, p. 101*
*Donovan, "Nominal", p. 158*

Speir, John
Port Roseway, 1783
Enslaved one person, Anna (age 20).
*Hodges, p. 69*

Spicer, (family of)
Parrsboro, dates unknown
Enslaved 'several'; details unknown.
*Whitfield, p. 222*

Stark (or Stork)
Granville Township, 1771
Enslaved one male, age and name unknown.
*Perkins, p. 131*

Starr (family of)
Parrsboro, dates unknown
Enslaved an unknown number of people; details unknown.
*Whitfield, p. 222*

Starr, Samuel
Cornwallis, 1786
Enslaved 'a few'; unknown names and ages.
*Whitfield, p. 216*

Stewart, John
Chedabucto, 1784
Enslaved two people, Elizabeth and Peter Dawson.
*Whitfield, p. 54*

Stogdon, (Widow)
Port Mouton, 1783
Enslaved one male, Peter Stogdon, age 19.
*Whitfield, p. 176*

Storer, John
Île Royale, 1745
Enslaved two males, Cato or Catto and Phillip Devotion.
*Donovan, "Nominal", p. 157*

St. Ovide (Governor)
Île Royale, 1728-29
Enslaved two male children, Charles Joseph and Jean Baptiste (both age 10).
*Donovan. "Nominal", p. 152*
*Whitfield, p 101*

Stuart, John
Shelburne, April 22, 1794
Enslaved one boy, unknown name. Described as "A Negro Boy".
*NS Archives Letter by James Cox regarding the case of a Negro boy*
*kidnapped in Liverpool and taken to the West Indies.*

Summers, William
Port Roseway, 1783
Enslaved one female, Poll. Age unknown.
*Whitfield, p. 147*

Sutherland, (Mr.)
Liverpool, 1777
Enslaved one male, name and age unknown.
*Diary of Simeon Perkins, p. 166*

Sutherland, Adam
Port Roseway, 1783
Enslaved one male, Adam (age 21).
*Hodges, Book Two, p. 147*

Symon, (Captain)
Tracadie, 1783
Enslaved one male, James Phillip (age 40).
*Whitfield, p. 144*
*Book of Negroes*


# T


Taylor, Courtenay
Port Roseway, 1783
Enslaved two people, including 1 female, Marrianne, age unknown.
*Whitfield, p. 119*

Taylor, John
Annapolis Royal, 1807
Enslaved six people; two females, two males and two children
Author of the petition
*Petition of John Taylor*

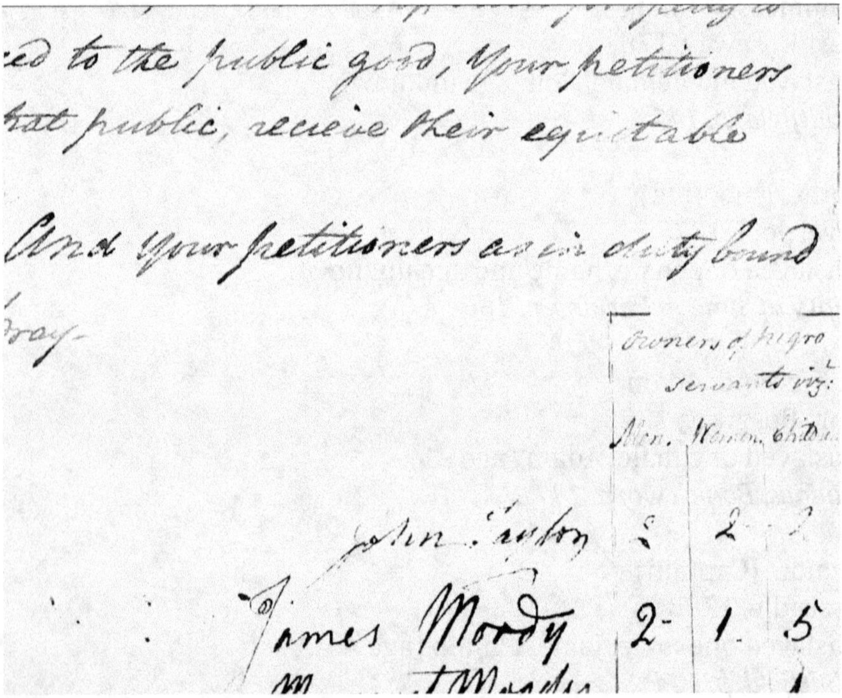
to the public good, Your petitioners
public, receive their equitable

And your petitioners as in duty bound

Owners of Negro servants viz:

Men. Women.

James Moody 2- 1. 5

*Figure 56: John Taylor's petition signature*
...at the head of Enslavers petitioning the Nova Scotia government.

*Nova Scotia Archives, Nova Scotia House of Assembly*
*RG 5 series A volume 14 number 49 (microfilm 15591)*

Taylor, William and Wesley (brothers)
Digby County, 1780s-90s
Shared the enslavement of one woman, Lucy.
*Whitfield, p. 117*

Thomas, George
Shelburne, 1783
Enslaved two females, Hannah and one other.
*Whitfield, p. 78*
*Book of Negroes*

Thomas, John
Shelburne, unknown dates
Enslaved one person, details unknown.
*Whitfield, p. 223*

Thomas, Thomas
Halifax, 1752
Enslaved one male, Orange, age unknown.
*Whitfield, p. 140*
*Smith, p. 9*

Thorne, Edward
Annapolis County, 1807
Enslaved two people, one male and one female. Unknown names but believed to have the surname of Jackson, as an African Nova Scotian family by that surname lived there in the 1790s.
*Petition of John Taylor*

Timpany, Robert
Digby, 1780s
Enslaved five people, details unknown.
*Harris, p. 7*

Tippert, Gilbert
Port Roseway, 1783
Enslaved two children, one male, Joe (age 10) and Nancy (11).
Book of Negroes
*Whitfield, pp. 103-104, 134*

Todd, John
Chedabucto, 1783
Recorded as having enslaved 'several'; known names are Ann,
Curry, March, Prime, Susannah.
*Whitfield, pp. 15, 118, 151, 178*

Tonge, Walter
Windsor Township (Eastern District), 1794
Enslaved one male, William.
*States, p. 46*

Tonge, William Cottnam
Windsor/Hants County, 1790s
Enslaved one male, Walter.
*Frost and States, Section 3, p. 38*

Totten, Joseph
And daughters Phebe, Mary and Jane Totten
Annapolis County, 1788
Enslaved Harry (age 12) and Peter (28) along with
other children; known names are Bella, Clarinda and Silvia
*Whitfield, pp. 20, 171*
*Hodges, Book One, page 56*

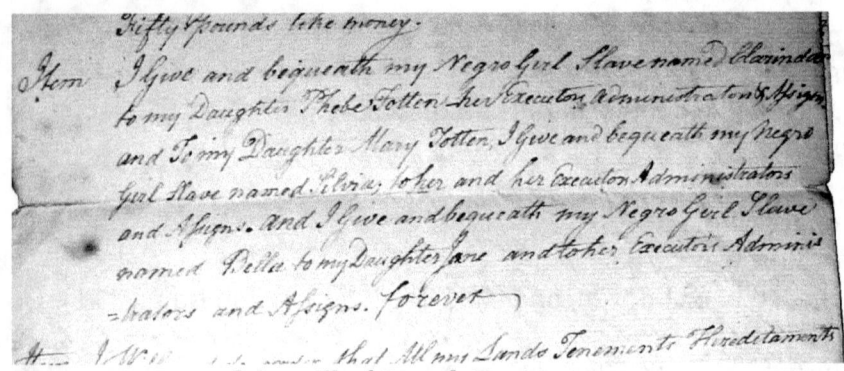

*Figure 57: Part of the will of Joseph Totten*
"Item - I give and bequeath my negro girl slave Clarinda to my
daughter Phebe Totten...and to my daughter Mary Totten...my

negro slave girl named Silvia...I give my negro slave girl named Bella to my daughter Jane."

*archives.novascotia.ca/africanns/archives/?ID=4*

Townsend, Gregory, Esq.
Halifax, 1786
Enslaved two people; Nancy, whom he purchased from Abraham Forst, and her child.
*Smith, pp. 50-51*

Townsend, Richard
Shelburne, 1791
Enslaved two males, Isaac Luther (age 20) and another.
P. Parker was supposed to hand Isaac over to Townsend or Hill.
*Whitfield p. 117*

Trigler, Edward
Port Roseway, 1783
Enslaved one male, Prince Fraction.
*Whitfield, p. 71*

Tritton, (Mrs.)
Cornwallis Township, 1806
Enslaved one child, Lois. Age unknown.
*Whitfield, p. 115*

Troop, Jacob
Annapolis County, 1805
Enslaved one female child, Hannah (age 11).
*Whitfield, p. 80*

> Will of Jacob Troop 1805
> "At the death of my beloved wife Anna, the black girl Hannah, if she served as a faithful servant till she is 30 years of age, she is to have her freedom but if she is not 30 years of age at the death of my beloved wife Anna, then her service

is to be divided equally among my five daughters till she arrives at the age of 30, being 11 years of age."

*Perkins, p. 138*

Tucker, Reuben
Digby County, dates unknown
Enslaved one male, Frances. Age unknown.
*Whitfield, p. 71*

Turner, John
Port Roseway, 1783
"Indentured" one person for 10 years, Grace (age 7).
*Hodges, Book Two, p. 147*

# U

Uniacke, Martha (married to Richard John Uniacke, Attorney General of Nova Scotia)
Halifax, 1770
Enslaved one child, mulatto John Patten, whom she inherited from Martha Pritchard of Halifax.

Urion, (or Union) Miles
Digby township, 1787
Enslaved one male, London, age 18.
*Whitfield, p. 115*

# V

VanBuskirk, first name unknown
Annapolis County, 1783
Enslaved two people, Dinah and Robert. Ages unknown.
*Book of Negroes*
*Whitfield, pp. 61, 161*

VanDyke, John (Major)
Weymouth, 1783
Enslaved one male, Ned, age 20.
*Whitfield, p. 136*
*Book of Negroes*

VanHorne, Irene
Yarmouth, 1783
Enslaved one female, Judith, age 40.
*Book of Negroes*
*Whitfield, p. 108*

VanHorne, Lawrence
Colchester County, 1783
Enslaved one male, Sam, age 22.
*Whitfield, pp. 165-6*

Vanshant, Albert
Shelburne, 1783
Enslaved one female, Lucy, age 16.
*Whitfield, p. 116*
*Book of Negroes*

VanWinkle, John
Port Roseway, 1783
Enslaved four people: one male William Etherington (age 13), one female, Mary (36) Jackey (3) and Sally (6 months).
*Book of Negroes*
*Whitfield, p. 66*

Villejoint (family of)
Île Royale, 1754
Enslaved one female, Marie. Age unknown.
*Donovan, "Nominal", p.157*
*Whitfield, p. 119*

Vroom, John
Annapolis/Digby County, 1807
Enslaved six people, including three females, one male and one child. All names and ages unknown.
*Petition of John Taylor*


# W


Waldron, (Ensign)
Country Harbour, 1784
Enslaved one female, Patty. Age unknown.
*Whitfield, p. 140*

Walker, (family of)
Wilmot, 1787
Enslaved two females, Charlotte and Nancy. Ages unknown.
*Whitfield, p. 42*

Wall, Patrick
Port Mouton, 1783
Enslaved one child, Letitia, age 5.
*Whitfield, p. 113*
*Book of Negroes*

Wallace, Michael (the Honourable)
Sable Island, 1809
Enslaved one man, Prince, who was offered to him by James Morris.
*See letter under Morris, James.*

*See next page.*

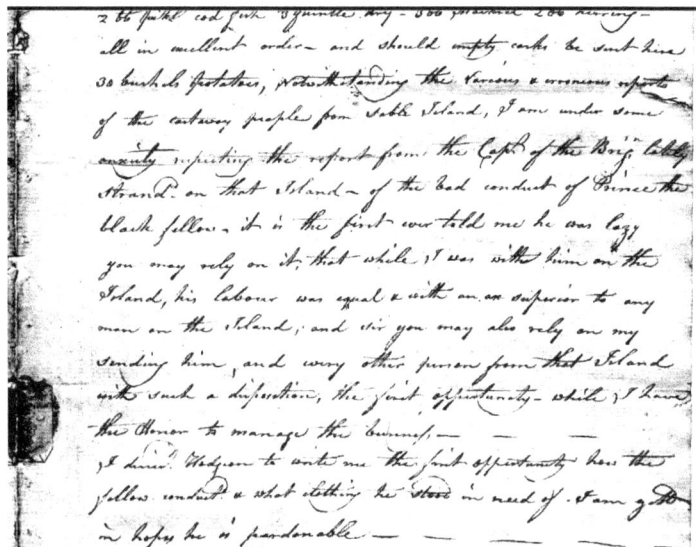

*Figure 58: Letter from Michael Wallace*

"Notwithstanding the various & erroneous reports of the castaway people from Sable Island, I am under some anxiety respecting the report from the Capt. of the Brig lately Stranded on that Island of the bad conduct of Prince the black fellow, it is the first ever told me he was lazy you may rely on it that while I was with him on the Island, his about was equal and with an one superior to any man on the Island..."

*Nova Scotia Archives RG 1 volume 425 number 1*

Wallace, Michael
Nova Scotia/Sable Island, 1794-1806
Enslaved one male, Belfast aka Bill.
*Whitfield, p. 25-26*

*See next page.*

# Twenty Dollars Reward.

RAN Away, on Thurſday evening, the 18th inſt. a Negro Man Servant, the property of the Subſcriber, named BEL-FAST ; but who commonly goes by the name of BILL.————At the time of he elopement he was in the ſervice of William Forſyth, Eſq ; and had mediated an attempt to get on board a ſhip that night which lay in the harbour, bound to Newfoundland ; but was fruſtrated : It is probable, however, he may ſtill endeavour to eſcape that way, therefore, the maſters of all coaſters going along ſhore, or other veſſels bound to ſea, are hereby forewarned from carrying him off at their peril, as they will be proſecuted, if diſcovered, with the utmoſt rigour of the law.

The above reward will be paid to any perſon or perſons who ſhall apprehend and ſecure him, ſo that I may recover him again.

He is a likely, ſtout-made fellow, of five feet eight or nine inches high, and about 27 years of age ; of a mild good countenance and features, ſmooth black ſkin, with very white teeth ; is a native of South Carolina, ſpeaks good Engliſh, and very ſoftly, and has been in this Province ten years.

When he went off, he wore an old Bath-Coating ſhort coat, of a light colour, wore out at the elbows ; brown cloth or duffil trowſers, alſo much wore at the knees ; a round hat, and an old black ſilk handkerchief about his neck :—But as he had other cloaths ſecreted in town, he may have changed his whole apparel.

He will no doubt endeavour to paſs for a free man, and poſſibly by ſome other name.

## MICHAEL WALLACE.

*Figure 59: Reward offered*
...for a slave named Belfast ,who ran away from Michael Wallace.
*Weekly Chronicle, 15 March 1794  NS Archives microfilm 8165*

Ward, Moses
Annapolis County, 1783
Enslaved one female child, Sibbe, age 11.
*Whitfield, p. 170*

Ward, Ebenezer
Annapolis Royal, 1783
Enslaved one female child, Eliza Ward, age 7.
*Hodges, Book Two, p. 146*

Wenman, Richard
Halifax, 1781 (September)
Enslaved one man, Cato, age unknown.
*Smith, p. 91*

> "give unto my Negro named Cato his liberty...and herby [sic]
> release him from all idea of slavery if he will faithfull [sic]
> serve my said daughter, Elizabeth Susanna Pringle, two
> years and not otherwise."
>
> *Smith p. 91*

Wentworth, John (Lieutenant Governor)
Halifax, 1784
Enslaved nineteen known people; Ann, Celia, Cyrus, Daphne,
Dorothy, Elenora, Henry, Isaac, James, January, John, Lymas, Mat-
thew, Priscilla, Quako, Rachel, Susannah, Venus, William.
Wentworth sent all 19 people to his brother, Paul Wentworth, in
Suriname.
*Wentworth Letters vol. 49 Feb. 24, 1784 NSA*
*Whitfield, pp. 178, 216*

Westphal, George
Cole Harbour, 1784
Enslaved six people, including Alexander, Ambrella, Colly, and
Lyddy.
*Whitfield, pp. 13, 117, 215, 229, 233*

Whidden, John
Cornwallis, 1788
Enslaved one female, Charlotte.
*Cornwallis Township Book NSA*

Whiting, Nathan
Île Royale, 1746
Enslaved one female, June Zabud. Age unknown
*Whitfield, p. 108*
*Donovan, "Nominal", p. 156*

Willbank(s), William
Port Roseway, 1783
Enslaved two people, one female, Lilliy, and one child, Leah. Ages unknown.
*Whitfield, p. 115*

Wilkins, Isaac
Shelburne, 1783
Enslaved 'several', names and ages unknown.
*Whitfield, p. 223*

> "...(Wilkins) is said to have brought a number of slaves to the beautiful spot on the shores of Shelburne harbor called by his family Ridge Vale, but popularly known for many years as 'Wilkins's Folly.'"
>
> *Smith, pp. 23-34*

Wilkins, Robert
Port Roseway, 1783
Enslaved one female, Dinah (age 26).
*Hodges, p. 69*

Williams, Ann
Annapolis Royal, 1771
Enslaved one male, unknown name and age
*Smith, "The Slave in Canada", p. 15*

Williams, Frederick
Annapolis County, 1807
Enslaved six people: two males, Prince and Unknown; one female, details unknown; and three children, names and ages unknown.
*Petition of John Taylor*
*Whitfield, p. 154*

Willet, Walter
Clementsport, 1797
Enslaved one male, Caesar Hawkins (who married Jane Japean).
*March 11, 1797 Granville Township Book NSA*

> "Tuesday, March 25th...Ceasar Hawkns began work....hired him for 6 months...(slave to Mr. Willet)"
> *Cousins, p. 73*

Wilkins, Robert
Shelburne, 1783
Enslaved one female, Dinah. Age unknown.
*Whitfield, p. 61*

Williams, Ann (wife of Thomas Williams)
Annapolis Royal, 1771
Enslaved one male, name and age unknown.
*Whitfield, p. 198*

Willoughby, Samuel
Cornwallis Township, 1783
Enslaved one female, unknown name and age.
*Whitfield, p. 225*

Wilson, John
Halifax, 1783
Enslaved one male, Ben, age unknown.
*Runaway slave ad Nova Scotia Gazette May 20, 1783*

Wilson, Joseph
Falmouth, 1764-1776
Enslaved three people; two females, Byna and Sylla, and one male, James.
*Smith, "The Slave in Canada", pp. 15, 234*

> "Recorded in the Falmouth Township Book on 24 March 1764, in relation to a proprietor's meeting, was the following: 'voted that one Axman should be chosen to assist the surveyor. Chosen James Wilson, a Black boy belonging to Joseph Wilson. Voted that the chairman and ax (sic) boy be paid 3 shillings a day for their labour."
>
> *States, p. 38*

Wilson, William
Cumberland County, 1783
Enslaved five people, including Ivey Hilley and Jacob aka Frank.
*Whitfield, pp. 90, 95*
*Book of Negroes*

Winslow, Edward
Halifax, 1784
Enslaved three men: Caesar, Frank, Juba. Ages unknown.
*Whitfield, p. 36*

Winniett, Joseph (Judge)
Annapolis/Digby, 1771-1807
Enslaved at least four people. Names and ages are unknown.
*Smith, "The Slave in Canada", p. 15*
*Petition of John Taylor and Other Slaveowners*
*Perkins, p. 131*

> "We can take it from the following story that Joseph Winni-
> ett was a kind-hearted man towards his servants. It is said
> that a slave girl had one day during Mr. Winniett's absence
> from home, provoked to the utmost the patience of her mis-
> tress. On his return Mrs. Winniett demanded a severe whip-
> ping for the slave at the hands of her master. Having
> ordered the girl to an adjoining room, Mr. Winniett charged
> her to scream at the top of her voice while he proceeded to
> apply his whip with such vigour to the furniture as to make
> everything rattle and then, at the opened door, the satisfied
> mistress informed the refractory girl that she had learned a
> lesson without any mistake this time!"
>
> *Perkins, p. 136*

Winniett, Magdalen
Annapolis Royal, 1771
Enslaved three people; one woman, one man and one child. Names
and ages unknown.
*Smith, "The Slave in Canada", p. 15*
*Whitfield, p. 224*

Wiswall, John (Reverend)
Wilmot, 1780s
Enslaved one known woman, Dinah.

> "Remember me to Dinah. I allow her to live with you or
> where she pleases  until she hears from me. I am determ-
> ined not to sell her to anybody."
>
> *Harris, p. 17*

Wright, (Dr.)
Halifax, 1783
Enslaved one person, Mercury, age 20.
*Whitfield, p. 125*
*Book of Negroes*

Wood, Francis
Shelburne, 1783
Enslaved four people: Elizabeth and her child; Jack (age 15) and Jude.
*Book of Negroes*
*Whitfield, pp. 65,91*

Wood, Mary (married to Reverend Thomas Wood)
Annapolis Royal, 1767
Enslaved one person, a 'mulatto' girl named Louisa. Purchased by Wood from Charles Proctor of Halifax, merchant, for £15.
*Perkins, p. 131*
*Whitfield, p. 116*

# Y

Young, Isaac (Captain)
Digby Township, 1783/84
Recorded as enslaving 'several' people. Only two known names are Charles and Pompey.
*Smith, p. 25*
*Whitfield, p. 148*

Young, John
Amherst, 1787
Enslaved one male, Michael Taylor.
*Will of John Young, Jan 1787 Abstract of Cumberland County Wills*

Young, William
Shelburne, 1784
Enslaved one male, Isaac. Age unknown.
*Whitfield, p. 89*
*General Sessions of Shelburne April 6, 1784 MG4*

===

42nd Regiment
Sydney, 1787
Enslaved three people, James and two others.
*Whitfield, p. 99*

Brenda J. Thompson

# Enslavers of New Brunswick

## A part of Nova Scotia until 1784
## Also known as Wabanaki

## A

Agnew, John (Reverend)
Saint John, 1792
Enslaved one male, Prince.
According to historian Otto Lorenz, Agnew left 36 enslaved people behind in Virginia.
*Runaway Ad in Royal Gazette June 17, 1788*
*Whitfield p. 153*

RANAWAY
FROM the SUBSCRIBER, on the 4th inst. A NEGRO MAN slave named PRINCE.—He carried off with him a new grey cloth coat with short skirts, and a lappelled waistcoat and trowsers of the same, all neatly made, and mounted with metal buttons—also a new coat of lighter grey, with metal buttons and long skirts—a new fox skin cap with a bushy tail, and a good hat—three good shirts—one of them very stout linen—a pair of good shoes, and a pair of new grey and purple coloured stockings, and a very good blue and black cloth coloured coat, mounted with silk chequered buttons, rather too large for him.

HE is artful, has a gloomy and malevolent look—is a daring liar, and has attempted twice before this to RUNAWAY.

ALL masters of vessels and others are hereby warned

against carrying said NEGRO out of the Province, entertaining, harbouring, or employing him in any manner—and whoever takes and secures said NEGRO in any GAOL in this Province, and gives information to Messrs. THOMSON & REID, Merchants, St. John, or the SUBSCRIBER in Maugerville, so that his master can recover him shall be handsomely REWARDED.
JOHN AGNEW
Maugerville, 5th May, 1792

*Saint John Gazette, 29 June 1792*
*Chute, "Runaway", p. 46*

Agnew, Stair (Judge)
Fredericton
1800
Enslaved one female, name and age unknown.

> "Jones, like Agnew, was a slave owner and they had been friends in 1800 when both were involved in court cases testing the legality of slavery in New Brunswick."
>
> *Dictionary of Canadian Biography*
> *biographi.ca/en/bio.php?id_nbr=2728*

Allen, Isaac (Judge)
New Brunswick (formerly of Wilmot, NS), 1780s
Enslaved more than seven people, all names and ages unknown.
*Whitfield, p. 225*
*Smith, p. 114*

Allen manumitted some of his slaves and sold some to Lawrence Hartshorne of Dartmouth, NS. Hartshorne ended up freeing all of his enslaved people.

> "Isaac Allen was a complicated loyalist. Although he owned upwards of seven African slaves at one time, he was a friend and champion of free blacks. During his time of service with

the New Jersey Volunteers in Charleston, South Carolina he met and befriended a Baptist minister who had once been a slave. Allen admired the loyalist guerilla leader, Colonel Tye, a man who had been enslaved in Pennsylvania.

At the revolution's end, Allen escorted a free black family to the mouth of the St. John River where he wrote a letter recommending that they be treated as other Loyalist refugees. Seven years later, although he was an Anglican and a slave owner, Allen helped his Baptist minister friend receive a license to preach in New Brunswick."

*Davidson, "Loyalist Trails"*

# B

Bailey, William
Saint John, possibly, 1783
Enslaved two people, Mary and Issac York, a married couple. They were involved in a court case.
*Whitfield, p. 124*

Bean, Thomas
Maugerville (possibly), 1787
Enslaved at least one person – Keziah/Kezzia, age 20.
*Whitfield, p. 111*

> Runaway Ad in *Royal Gazette*, August 21, 1787
> RUN-AWAY
> FROM the subscriber on Wednesday evening last the 15th instant, a negro woman named KEZIAH, about five feet high, has the marks of a cut and a burn, I believe, on her right cheek, near her mouth, took with her two calico gowns, one a white, the other a nankeen ground, the flowers running through it in stripes, also, a dark purple and white calico frisk and petticoat—has different short gowns, among which is a blue and white striped linen, and a white: Also, a white cloth cloak and a black bonnet lined with white,

covered in gauze, and lace hopped around the edge —
Whoever will apprehend and take up said negro woman, so
that her master may have her again, shall receive a reward
of TWO GUINEAS, and all reasonable charges paid.

All Masters of vessels and others are hereby forbid
carrying off the said Nego slave, as they will answer for it at
their peril.

Aug. 17th THOMAS BEAN

*Chute, p. 43*

Beardsley, John (Reverend)
Woodstock, 1783
Enslaved four people: Bazley, Scipio (age 30), Dinah (35) Peter
(24).
*Whitfield, p. 19*
*skirret.com/papers/canada/john_beardsley.html*

Beattie, Edward
New Brunswick, 1783
Enslaved three people: Betty (age 26) Sarah (11 mos.) and Jack (4).
*Book of Negroes*
*Whitfield, p. 24*

Bennison, George
New Brunswick, 1792
Enslaved mother and daughter, names unknown.
They were involved in a court case in New Brunswick.
*Whitfield p. 227*

Brown, D
New Brunswick, 1809
Enslaved at least one female, Nancy, age unknown.

FOR SALE,

A NEGRO WENCH, named NANCY, belonging to the Subscriber.— A good title will be given.
OCTOBER 6, 1809.                    D. BROWN.

*Royal Gazette, Oct.6, 1809*

# C.

Carey, John
New Brunswick, 1788
Enslaved one woman, name unknown, whom James Hayt
purchased.
This young woman ran away from James Hayt.

FOR SALE,
A stout, likely and very active
Young BLACK WOMAN,
late the property of John H. Carey;
She is not offered for any fault, but is
singularly sober and diligent.——
Enquire of JAMES HAYT.
October 3, 1788.

*Saint John Gazette & Weekly Advertiser, Oct. 3, 1788*

Carman, Richard
Maugerville, 1783
Enslaved one man, Ned (age 40).
*Book of Negroes*
*Whitfield p. 136*

Clarke, Joseph
Saint John, 1792
Enslaved four people: Statia (age 30), Richard (aka Dick) and
son(5), London.
*Whitfield p. 88*

> *Royal Gazette*, 17 August 1787
> RAN AWAY from the subscriber, the 19th of July last,
> LONDON, a negro boy, aged 18 years, had on when he went
> away a light colored coasting jacket, osnaburg trowsers,
> green bay shirt, with white sleeves, and wants the first
> joining of the second toe of the left foot. Whoever will
> apprehend the said negro and secure him, so that his
> master, may get him again, shall have ONE GUINEA Reward;
> and all masters of vessels and others are hereby forbid to
> carry him off, or to employ him as a servant or otherwise.
>     JOSEPH CLARKE
>
> *Chute, p. 42*

> *Saint John Gazette*, 29 June 1792
> Three Guineas Reward
> RAN-A-WAY
> From the Subscriber on the night of the 9th instant, an
> indented servant Man, named
> DICK HOPEWELL;
>     About 5 feet 9 inches high -- very active, and supposed to
> be near 40 years of age. --Had on when he went off a
> fearnought grey short coat and trowsers with white metal
> buttons --a new felt hat, &c.
>     At the same time went off a Negro Woman slave, named

STATIA

Who he claim'd as a Wife, with two small children—a boy about 5 years old and a girl about 15 months—she is about 30 years of age, and now pregnant.—Had on when she went a green duffle petticoat, with a baize short gown of the same colour—she is of the mulatto cast, and speaks very fluently.—Whoever will secure said RUN-AWAYS in any goal of this Province, or the Province of Nova Scotia, so that their master may recover them, shall be entitled to the above reward.

MASTERS of vessels and others are hereby cautioned not to harbour, conceal, or employ said RUNAWAYS, as they will be prosecuted to the utmost rigour of the law.
JOSEPH CLARKE
Maugerville, 14th June 1792.

*Chute, p. 45*

Coffin, John
New Brunswick. 1800
Enslaved one male,
David Prince, age
unknown.
*The Royal Gazette, 27
May 1800*

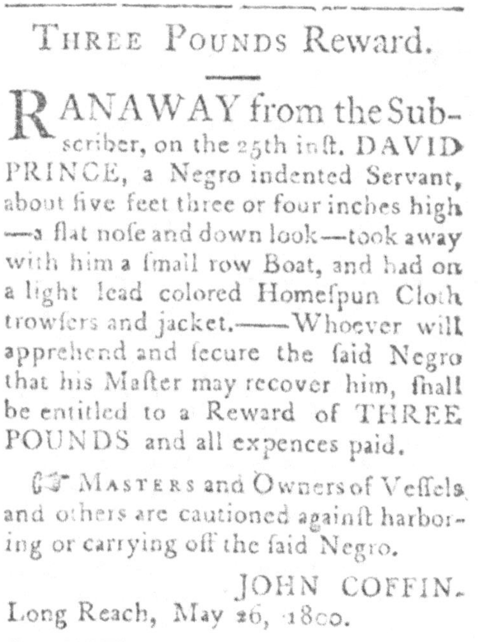

### THREE POUNDS Reward.

RANAWAY from the Subscriber, on the 25th inst. DAVID PRINCE, a Negro indented Servant, about five feet three or four inches high —a flat nose and down look—took away with him a small row Boat, and had on a light lead colored Homespun Cloth trowsers and jacket.——Whoever will apprehend and secure the said Negro that his Master may recover him, shall be entitled to a Reward of THREE POUNDS and all expences paid.

☞ MASTERS and Owners of Vessels and others are cautioned against harboring or carrying off the said Negro.

JOHN COFFIN.
Long Reach, May 26, 1800.

*Figure 60: "Ranaway" ad from John Coffin*

Cory, Sarah
Queens County, 1787-1815
Enslaved three people, Dorothy plus her two children, names
unknown.
*Chute, p. 42*

> Will of Sarah Corey, Queens County, 1815 PANB:
> The family's African slave, Dorothy, was now 36 years old
> and had children of her own. Her inheritance was perhaps
> the most valuable of the treasures that Sarah bequeathed.
> The widow's will declared that Dorothy and her family
> were "to be free from slavery with her bed and bedding and
> wearing clothing without any demands of my children".
> *Davidson, Stephen, "Loyalist Trails 2008-41"*
> *uelac.ca/loyalist-trails/loyalist-trails-2008-41/*

Crannell, Bartholomew (Judge)
Queen's County. 1783
Enslaved one male, Sam (age 35).
*Book of Negroes*
*Whitfield, p. 165*

# D.

Davis, Benjamin
Saint John, 1788
Enslaved one man, Prince.
*Whitfield, p. 153*

> *Royal Gazette*, 17 June 1788
> Three POUNDS REWARD
> RUN-AWAY, last night, a negro man named PRINCE, a stout
> well made fellow, about five feet eight inches high, has a
> sour down look; had on and took with him, a new blanket
> coat, a red short jacket, (the laps faced with green,) an old
> drab coating, a corduroy pair breeches, an old pair coating

trowsers, two new check shirts, one new pair of shoes, one pair of half boots, 2 black caps, one dog and the other bear skin, and one white hat. --WHOEVER will secure him in any jail in this province, or bring him to his master near Fredericton, shall have the above reward and all reasonable charges.

May 20th 1788

Benj. Davis

N.B. All Masters of vessels are forbid carrying him off, and all persons from harbouring or employing the above described fellow.

*Chute, p. 44*

de Peyster, Abraham
Maugerville, 1797
Enslaved two people,
Abraham and Lucy,
ages unknown.
*Whitfield p. 4*

*Figure 61: Abraham de Peyster*

*Image courtesy of Dictionary of Canadian Biography biographi.ca/en/bio/ de_peyster_abraham_4E.html*

Deveber, Gabriel
Sunbury County, 1827
Enslaved at least four people: James Head, Lucy and Abraham, Orthellow Hammon. Possibly enslaved Catherine Harrim, whom he referred to as "my black woman" in his will.
*Whitfield pp. 78, 80, 82, 117*

Dixon, Charles
Sackville, early1800s
Enslaved one person, Cleveland, who was set free in Dixon's will.
*Dictionary of Canadian Biography, Vol. 5*

> "To this end, he strove to set a Christian example by freeing his black slave Cleveland, whom he had purchased at Halifax for £60, offered financial assistance to the needy, helped build the first Sackville meeting-house, and donated land for a parsonage, providing in his will for its maintenance. He died at his home on 21 Aug. 1817, survived by his wife, three sons, and four daughters."

Donn/Dow, Van Dyne
New Brunswick, 1783
Enslaved two people, Jacob (age 12) and another, name unknown.
*Whitfield p. 95*
*Book of Negroes*

# E.

Ellegood, Jacob
York County, 1802
Enslaved "several" - known names are Betty, Irvin, John, Adam, Sally Wise.
*Will of Jacob Ellegood, 1802 PANB*
*Whitfield, pp. 24, 89, 235*

> "Jacob Ellegood was a Loyalist from Virginia who was used

to having a great number of enslaved Africans. At his death in 1802, his son Wiliam received 'all my Negroes except one wench called Better and one girl not above 12 years of age'. His granddaughter Rebecca was willed 'one Negro girl not above 12 years of age to be chosen by her'. His son Jacob Junior was to receive his 'Negro boy John'. His son John was to be granted his 'mulatto wench Pleasant and her three children, James, Sally, and William'. Finally, son Samuel Ellegood was to be given a slave referred to as his 'Negro boy Irvin'.

*Davidson, Stephen, Loyalist Trails 2019-42: October 20, 2019 uelac.ca/loyalist-trails/loyalist-trails-2019-42/#Slaveowners*

# G.

Goodman, Isaac
Saint John, 1783
Enslaved one child, Charles (age 11)
*Book of Negroes*

Gutherie, Robert
King's County, 1797
Enslaved one known person, Bob, age unknown.
*Chute, p. 49*
*Saint John Gazette, Jan. 6, 1797*

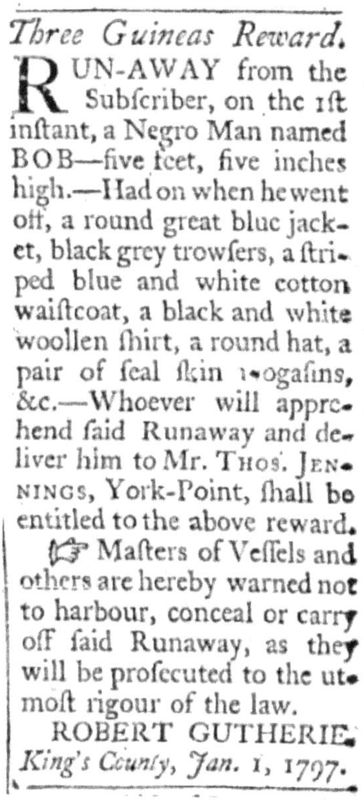

*Three Guineas Reward.*

RUN-AWAY from the Subscriber, on the 1st instant, a Negro Man named BOB—five feet, five inches high.—Had on when he went off, a round great blue jacket, black grey trowsers, a striped blue and white cotton waistcoat, a black and white woollen shirt, a round hat, a pair of seal skin mogasins, &c.—Whoever will apprehend said Runaway and deliver him to Mr. Thos. Jennings, York-Point, shall be entitled to the above reward.

☞ Masters of Vessels and others are hereby warned not to harbour, conceal or carry off said Runaway, as they will be prosecuted to the utmost rigour of the law.

ROBERT GUTHERIE,
*King's County, Jan. 1, 1797.*

*Figure 62: Robert Gutherie runaway slave ad*

# H.

Hall, John (Captain)
St. Andrews, 1787
Enslaved one male, Abraham, whom he sold to James Hayt.
Abraham consequently ran away from James Hayt. *See Hayt, James.*
*Whitfield, p. 9-10*

Hall, Peter
New Brunswick  (his adult children settled in Clements township, NS), 1792
Enslaved two females, a mother and daughter, names unknown.
*Peter Hall vs. George Bennison Court Case*
*Whitfield, p. 227*

Hallet, Samuel
Saint John County, 1795
Enslaved one known person, Phillis
*Book of Negroes*
*Whitfield, p. 145*

Harding, George
Maugerville, 1797
Enslaved one known person, Sippeo, later sold to George Harding's son.
*Whitfield, p. 174*

*See next page.*

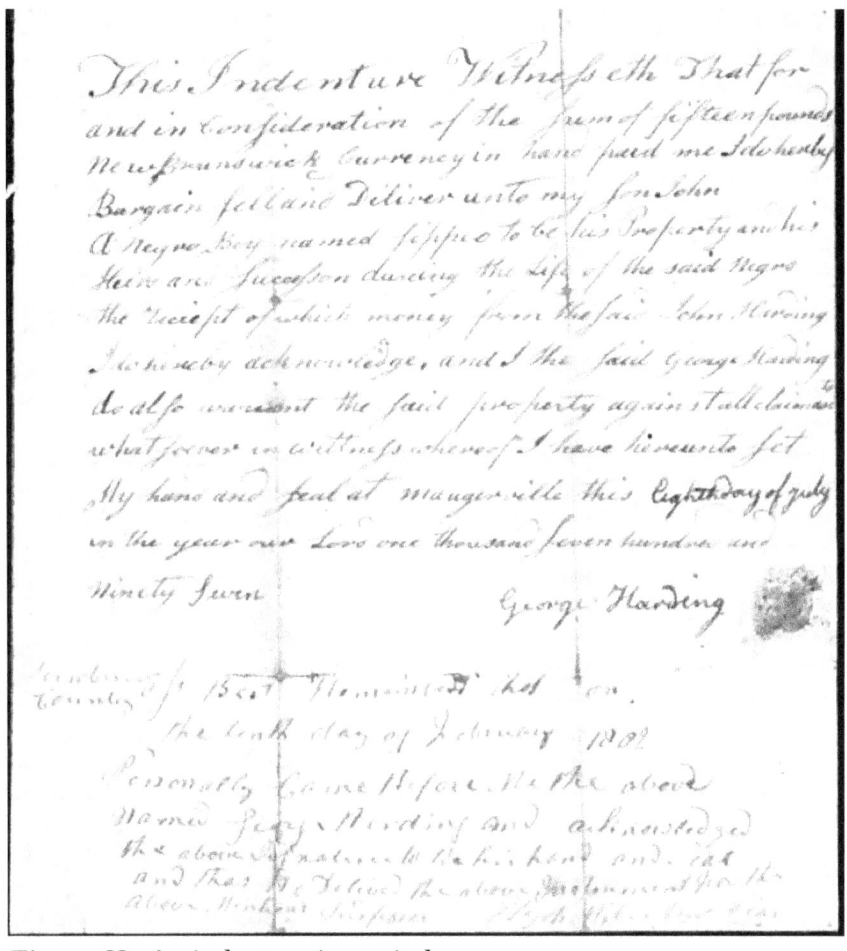

*Figure 63: An indenture in a window*
UNB Libraries - Black Loyalists in New Brunswick
preserve.lib.unb.ca/wayback/20141205155439/
atlanticportal.hil.unb.ca/acva/blackloyalists/
en/context/gallery/indenture.html

"An August 1890 *Daily Sun* article reported that Fredericton's citizens could see a photograph of a slave transfer in the window of Burkhard's photo shop. Major George Harding, a loyalist, sold a black named Sippeo to his son John Harding in 1797 for fifteen pounds. To insure that his son would have the benefits of

Sippeo's service, Harding had an indenture witnessed by Col. Elijah Miles, a local justice of the peace."

> Davidson, Stephen "Loyalist Trails 2018-09"
> uelac.ca/loyalist-trails/loyalist-trails-2018-09/

Harrison, Charles
Sunbury County, 1800
Enslaved one known person, Robert.
*Will of Charles Harrison, PANB* - Left £10 to his "old Servant Negroe Robert".
*Whitfield, p. 161*

> "...a Loyalist from New Jersey named Charles Harrison divided up his worldly possessions among his children, including his 'old servant Negro'. The latter was not identified by name but was, instead, noted for his monetary value – £10."
>
> Davidson, Stephen "Loyalist Trails 2018-09"
> uelac.ca/loyalist-trails/loyalist-trails-2018-09/

Hayt, James
New Brunswick, 1787
Enslaved Abraham (age 16) and a woman, name and age unknown.
See also John H. Carey "For Sale" advertisement of "A Stout, likely and Very Active Young Black Woman".
*Whitfield, pp. 9-10*

*See next page.*

# SIXTEEN DOLLARS REWARD,

AND all reasonable charges will be paid by JAMES HAYT, to any person who will detect and return ABRAHAM, a Run-Away negro boy, about 16 years of age—he had on a short blue jacket, with sleeves lined with white swan skin, a scarlet waistcoat, two rows bright buttons, with a collar, nankeen breeches, thread stockings, new shoes, plated buckles, and a small round black hat.—He has a pleasant countenance, is very talkative, tall of his age, but well proportioned, and formerly belonged to Capt. JOHN HALL, of Saint Andrews.      JAMES HAYT.
   September 12th, 1787.

*Figure 64: Ad for Abraham, a runaway*
...in the *Saint John Gazette*, 19 October, 1787

*Chute, p. 43*

Hecht, Frederick William
New Brunswick, 1784
Enslaved one male, Hector.
Hector was possibly from the Caribbean.
*Chute, p. 37*
*See next page.*

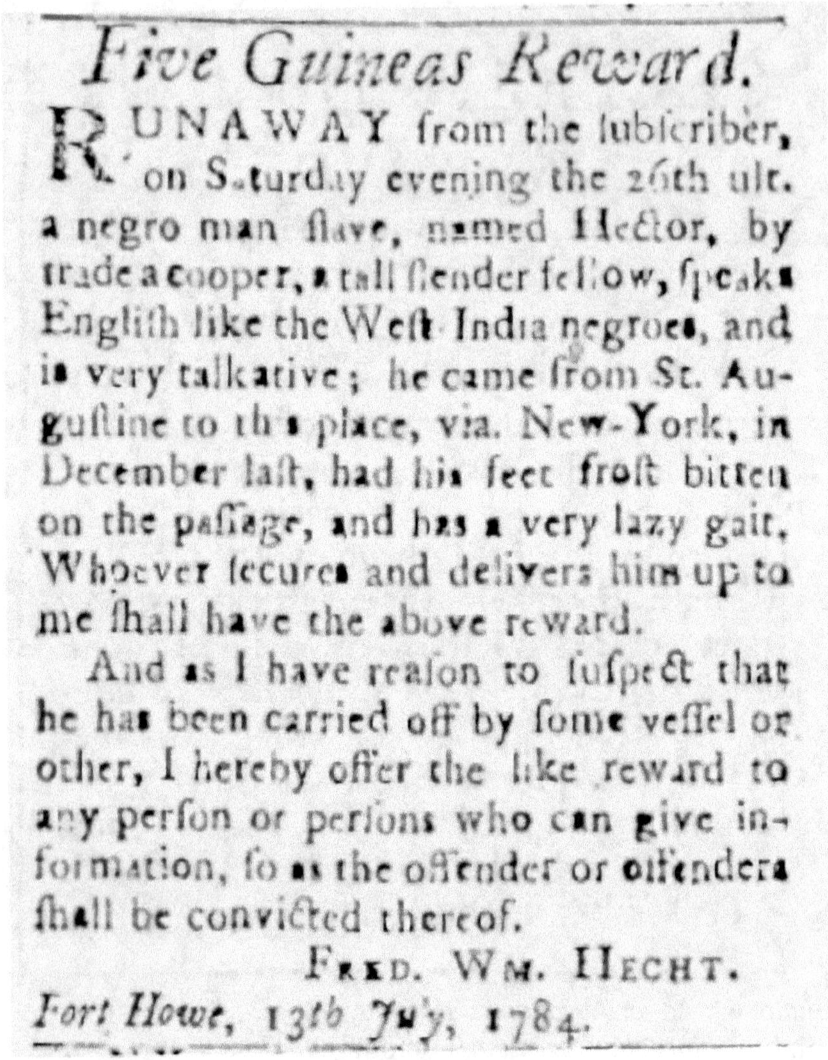

## Five Guineas Reward.

RUNAWAY from the subscriber, on Saturday evening the 26th ult. a negro man slave, named Hector, by trade a cooper, a tall slender fellow, speaks English like the West-India negroes, and is very talkative; he came from St. Augustine to this place, via. New-York, in December last, had his feet frost bitten on the passage, and has a very lazy gait. Whoever secures and delivers him up to me shall have the above reward.

And as I have reason to suspect that he has been carried off by some vessel or other, I hereby offer the like reward to any person or persons who can give information, so as the offender or offenders shall be convicted thereof.

FRED. WM. HECHT.

*Fort Howe,* 13th *July,* 1784.

*Figure 65: Ad for Hector, a runaway*
...in the *Saint John Gazette,* 15 July, 1784

Hillyard, Gersham
Saint John, 1786
Enslaved one male, Moses.
*Whitfield p. 130*

An article written in the *Royal Gazette*, June 13, 1783 notes that
Moses stole some food from his owner's store and when
neighbours chased him, Moses jumped off the wharf into the water,
where he drowned.

Hubbard, Nat
New Brunswick, 1783-84
Enslaved one male, Peter Cox (aka Cocks).
Peter ran away with Charity Morris and her child Edward Morris
along with Unus/Eanus Deaton (age 27).
　　Unus/Eanus is described in *The Book of Negroes* as "quadroon"
(one of her four grandparents was African-American) and "sickly".
　　It is not known if they were caught.
*Royal Saint John Gazette* May 13, 1784 Runaway Ad

Hughes, John
New Brunswick, 1785
Enslaved at least one female, name unknown (age 18).
An attempt was made to sell her at a public auction.
*Whitfield, p. 226*

Hume, John
Carriacou, 1785
Enslaved two people, Betty Hume and her son by a rape by John
Hume.
*Smith, p. 61*
*Whitfield, p. 89*

# J.

Jarvis, Munson
Saint John, 1797
Enslaved two people, Abraham and Lucy, whom he sold to
Abraham de Peyster.
*Whitfield, p. 4*

Jarvis, Samuel
St. John County, dates unknown
Enslaved at least four people, Zimri Armstrong and his wife and
children.

Zimri petitioned the New Brunswick Governor, unsuccessfully, for
his family's freedom.
*Whitfield p. 16*

Jones, Caleb
York County, 1786
Enslaved at least three people, including Flora (age 27) Nancy
(24), and Lidge.
*Whitfield p. 90;134-135*

> Royal Gazette, 25 July 1786
> RAN AWAY
> FROM the subscriber living at the Nashwakshis, in the
> county of York, between the 15th and the 21st days of this
> Instant July [June?], the following bound Negro slaves, vi.,
> ISAAC about 30 years old, born on Long Island near New-
> York, had on when he went away, a short blue coast, round
> hat and white trowsers.(sic) BEN, about 35 years old, had
> on a Devonshire Kersey jacket lined with Scotch plaid,
> corduroy breeches, and round hat. FLORA, a wench about
> 27 years old, much pitted with the small-pox, she had on a
> white cotton jacket and petticoat. ALSO NANCY about 24
> years old, who took with her a Negro child, about four years

old called LIDGE. The four last mentioned Negroes were born in Maryland, and lately brought to this country.

All Person are hereby forbid to harbour any of the above Negroes, and all masters of vessels are forbid to take any of them on board their vessel as they shall answer the consequences. A REWARD of TWO GUINEAS, shall be paid for each of the men, and SIX DOLLARS for each Negro woman, by Mr. THOMAS JENNINGS if taken and deliver'd to the said JENNINGS, or to the Subscriber in York County, the like reward with all reasonable charges will be paid by the said JENNINGS or the subscriber.

CALEB JONES
24 June 1786

*Chute, p. 40*

Jones, (Captain) near Fredericton, 1786 Enslaved two known people, Ben (30) and Lidge.

The court case of Nancy, owned by Captain Jones. Reported in *The Royal Gazette*, February 8, 1800

*See next page.*

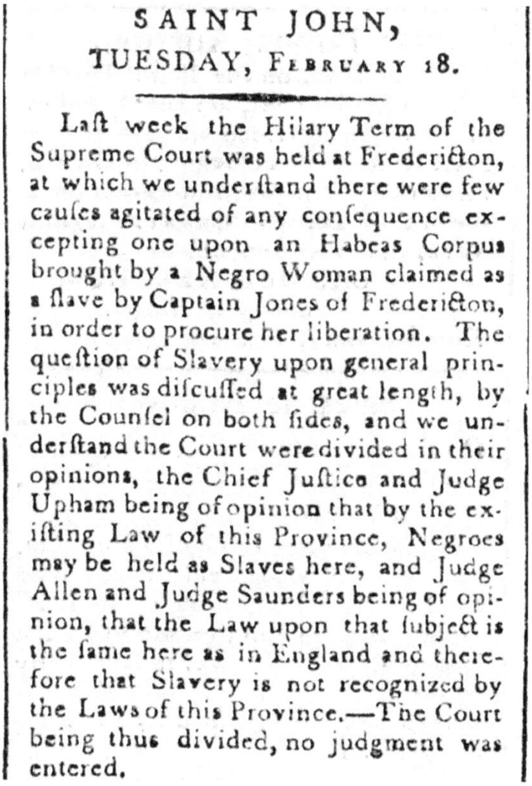

**SAINT JOHN, TUESDAY, FEBRUARY 18.**

Last week the Hilary Term of the Supreme Court was held at Frederiƈton, at which we underſtand there were few cauſes agitated of any conſequence excepting one upon an Habeas Corpus brought by a Negro Woman claimed as a ſlave by Captain Jones of Frederiƈton, in order to procure her liberation. The queſtion of Slavery upon general principles was diſcuſſed at great length, by the Counſel on both ſides, and we underſtand the Court were divided in their opinions, the Chief Juſtice and Judge Upham being of opinion that by the exiſting Law of this Province, Negroes may be held as Slaves here, and Judge Allen and Judge Saunders being of opinion, that the Law upon that ſubjeƈt is the ſame here as in England and therefore that Slavery is not recognized by the Laws of this Province.—The Court being thus divided, no judgment was entered.

*Figure 66: A court case about slavery*

"By the beginning of the 19th century there were a number of people in New Brunswick interested in the abolition of slavery and in February 1800 Jones became involved in an attempt to test its legality in the province. When a woman named Nancy (Ann), whom Jones was detaining as a slave, claimed her freedom, a writ of habeas corpus was issued and the case was presented to the full bench of the Supreme Court...Since the bench was equally divided, no judgement was recorded and the slave was returned to her master."

biographi.ca/en/bio/jones_caleb_5E.html

RUN away, a negro man named BEN, about thirty years of age, the property of Capt. Jones, had on when he went away a light brown jacket, a plaid (sic) waistcoat, corduroy breeches, white stockings, and a rough hat; is about five feet six inches high, stout and well set, has very black thick lips. Whoever takes up the said negro and delivers him to James Moore near Fredericton, or, secures him that the owner may get him again, shall have the above reward, and all the reasonable charges paid.

*The Royal Gazette and New Brunswick Advertiser*
(Saint John) 7 March 1786

Twelve Dollars Reward
RUN AWAY from the Subscriber
On the night of 15th June, a Negro Slave, called LIDGE, under five feet high, broad face and very large lips; brought him from Maryland with my family—he took with him a large CANOE with a Lathe across her; tared on the outside of the head with raw Tar, which looks red—he was seen going down the River. Any person that shall apprehend him and get the canoe, shall receive the above reward.
CALEB JONES

*The Royal Gazette*, 9 July 1816
*Chute, pp. 39, 51*

Jones, High
New Brunswick, 1785
Enslaved one female, name unknown.

A court case involved this enslaved woman. Jones allegedly sold a 'certain Negro Woman Slave' to Thomas Mullen but then Jones died before Mullen could claim the woman. A court case ensued, *Mullen vs. Lovitt (PANB)*
*Whitfield, p. 226*


# K.

Ketchim, John
Woodstock, 1783
Enslaved one known person, Phillis Ketchim (44)
*Book of Negroes*
*Whitfield p. 110*

Knapp, Titus
Westmoreland, 1808
Enslaved at least two people, Nero (27) and Baccus (13).
*Chute, p. 49*
*Whitfield, p. 18*

> "Nero ran away and Knapp put a Runaway Ad in the newspaper. Knapp was a well known dealer in Slaves and, after this advertisement, continued to sell and buy enslaved people for the next 13 years."
> *Loyalist Trails uelac.ca/loyalist-trails/loyalist-trails-2020-44/*

*See next page.*

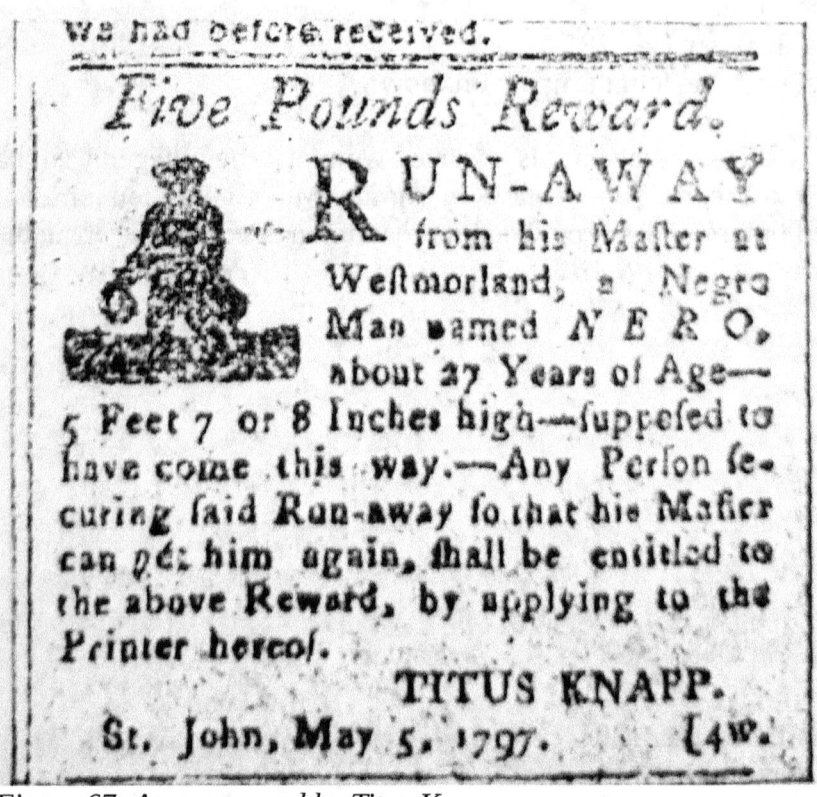

*Figure 67: A runaway ad by Titus Knapp*

## L.

Lawton, (Mr.)
Maugerville, 1797
Enslaved at several people, including one named either Elizabeth or Ester.
These women were baptized in New Brunswick and are listed as "Black Adults of Mr. Lawton and Mr. Longmire."
*Whitfield, p. 64*

Leonard, George
New Brunswick, 1780s
Enslaved two females, Eve and her daughter Sukey.
*Whitfield, p. 67*

Lester, Benjamin
Woodstock, 1783
Enslaved two people, Leititia (age 25) and Sam (15).
*Book of Negroes*
*Whitfield, pp. 113, 166*

Lester, Thomas
Waterborough
Enslaved at least two people, Beller (age 16) and his brother Sam.
They ran away with Tony Smith, a free man.
*Whitfield p. 20;166*

*Royal Gazette*, 10 July 1787
RUN-AWAY
IN a BIRCH CANOE, from the subscriber two negro Men and
one Wench; who have taken sundry things with them. SAM,
being a black and dark Mulatto 17 or 18 years old, midling
tall and slim; quick spoken, attempts to play the VIOLIN, has
a London brown coloured coat, ticking trousers and other
clothes.

BELLER, a sister to SAM, between a black and mulatto,
16 years old, midling tall and slim, is raw bon'd and has a
scar between her eye and temple, is slow in her speech, has
a black cover'd hat with white lining, and lived formerly
with Judge Peters at Saint John.

TONY SMITH, some call him JOE, a free fellow, but hired
for a time; he is tall and slim, between a black and mulatto,
speaks broken, wears blue or brown coat, ticking trousers,
and has other clothes with him. - Two of the above servants
were raised in the family. Any person apprehending them or
giving information to Mr. EZRA SCOFIELD, in King Street, St.

John, or the subscriber, shall have One GUINEA for each, and if taken out of St. John, reasonable charges paid—if taken out of the province, it is requested that they may be confined in Jail until called for. All masters of vessels and every other person is forewarned not to carry any of the said negroes off or from harbouring or concealing them, as they will answer it at their peril.
THOMAS LESTER
Waterborough, 19th June 1787

*Chute, p. 42*

Longmire, (Mr.)
New Brunswick
Enslaved several people, one being named Elizabeth or Ester. These women were baptized in New Brunswick and are listed as "Black Adults of Mr. Lawton and Mr. Longmire."
*Whitfield, p. 64*

Ludlow, (Colonel)
New Brunswick, dates unknown
Enslaved at least two females, Lydia and Maria.
*Smith, p. 86*
*Whitfield, p. 117*

# M.

McKay, (Captain)
New Brunswick, 1785
Enslaved one person, name unknown. Described as "Old".
*Wright, p. 97*
*Whitfield, p. 226*

McPherson, Charles
Saint John, 1793
Enslaved at least one male, Peter Thompson/Thomson.
Peter purchased his own freedom from McPherson.
*Whitfield, p. 181*

Menzies, (Major)
Musquash, 1783
Enslaved one child, Melinda (age 11).
*Book of Negroes*
*Whitfield, p. 125*

Miles, Elijah
New Brunswick, 1790s
Enslaved at least one person, name unknown.
Miles was a Magistrate and Politician in New Brunswick.
*biographi.ca/en/bio/miles_elijah_6E.html*
*Whitfield, p. 199*
*Smith, p. 86*

Millidge, Stephen
New Brunswick, 1791
Enslaved two people, Isaac and Rose (age 19).
Isaac was mentioned in a letter to Sarah Botsford Millidge.
*Whitfield pp. 90, 162*

Mills, Jonathan
Shediac (possibly), 1783
Enslaved a family of five; Charity and Edward Morris and their
three children.
A Runaway advertisement was placed in the *Saint John Gazette*
May 13, 1784. The family was re-enslaved.
*Whitfield, p. 129*

Morton, Alexander
Saint John, 1791
Enslaved one known person, Poll.
*Chute, p. 44*

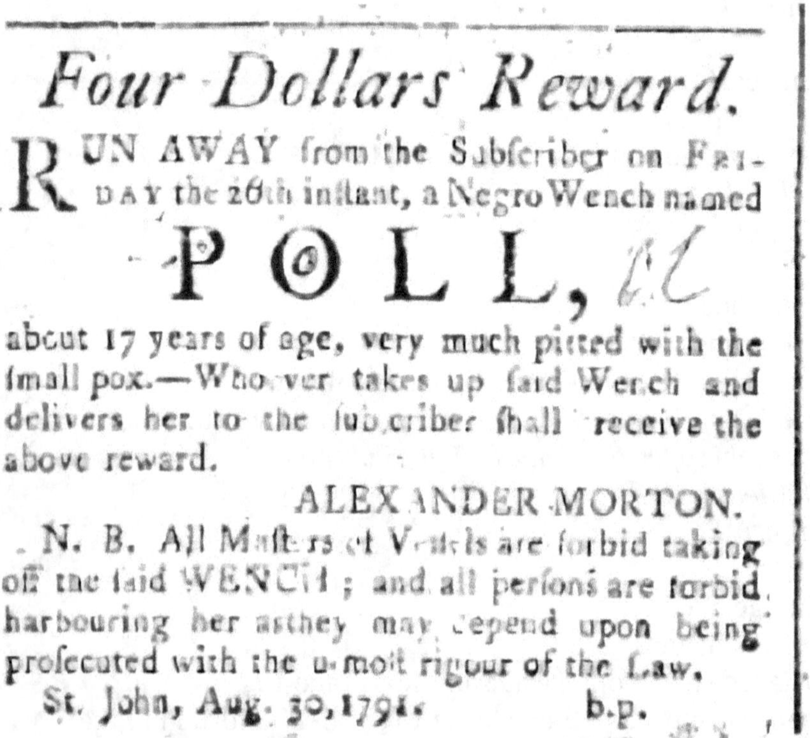

## Four Dollars Reward.

RUN AWAY from the Subscriber on Friday the 26th instant, a Negro Wench named

## POLL, *b.c*

about 17 years of age, very much pitted with the small pox.—Whoever takes up said Wench and delivers her to the subscriber shall receive the above reward.

ALEXANDER MORTON.

N. B. All Masters of Vessels are forbid taking off the said WENCH ; and all persons are forbid harbouring her as they may depend upon being prosecuted with the utmost rigour of the Law.

St. John, Aug. 30, 1791.                    b.p.

*Figure 68: Ad for a runaway named Poll
...in the Saint John Gazette, 30 September 1791*

Mount, John
New Brunswick, 1818
Enslaved one known person, Samuel Hutchings.
A Runaway Advertisement was placed for Samuel in the *New Brunswick Courier* on September 5, 1818.

Mullen/Mullins, Thomas
New Brunswick, 1785
Enslaved, possibly, one woman.
Thomas purchased one woman from High Jones, however, Jones died before Thomas could take possession of the woman. A court case ensued regarding the estate of High Jones.
*Mullen v. Lovitt, 1785 (PANB)*
*Whitfield, p. 226*

# O.

O'Dell, Jonathan
Frederick-town, 1780s
Enslaved "several", all names unknown.
Whitfield notes that some historians do not believe that O'Dell owned slaves and asserts this needs to be more thoroughly researched.
*Whitfield, p. 188*

*Figure 69: The O'Dell House in Fredericton*
Public Archives of New Brunswick (PANB #P5-272) says the ell on the back of the house was built as  slave quarters. This ell was removed in the 1950s.

# P.

Peters, James
Gagetown, Queens County, 1783-1799
Enslaved three people, Cairo, Gill, Dick
Gill and Dick ran away together.
*Book of Negroes*
*Whitfield p. 35*
*Will of James Peters, 1806, PANB*

> *Royal Gazette*, 20 August 1799
> Five Guineas Reward
> RANAWAY on Sunday the 11th instant, two Negro Men
> named GILL and DICK, the property of the subscribers.—
> GILL is a dark mulatto, with short wooly hair; is about five
> feet six inches high; stout made; has square shoulders, bow
> legs, and walks clumsily.—Had on when he went away a
> homespun coat, and vest a mixture of black and white, half
> lapelled; trowsers twilled homespun, a smutty brown, and
> considerably worn—he also took with him two striped
> vests, and sundry other articles of clothing.
>
> DICK is a short thick set fellow, about 5 feet 4 inches
> high; remarkably black; has a scar on his cheek and another
> on his chin.—He had on and took with him a variety of
> clothing--among other articles, a short coat without skirts;
> the color a mixture of blue with hemlock; nankeen overalls
> &c.,
>
> Whoever will apprehend and secure the said Runaways
> so that they may be had, shall be entitled to the above
> reward, or Three Guineas for either of them separately.
> REUBEN WILLIAMS
> JAMES PETERS
> Gagetown, August 20 1799
>
> *Chute, p. 50*

*See next page.*

"James Peters, a loyalist bound for the St. John River, had a slave named Cairo. She was married to a free Black Loyalist named Pompey Rumney."

*Davidson, Stephen Carleton's Book of Negroes:*
*A Ledger's Legacy (Part 2) Loyalist Trails 2016-35*
*uelac.ca/loyalist-trails/loyalist-trails-2016-35/#CarletonBook*

Pritchard, Azariah
New Brunswick, 1794
Enslaved one known person, Charles.
*Whitfield, p. 40*

# R.

Robinson, Beverly
New Brunswick, 1784
Enslaved 'at least 10', all names unknown.
*Smith, p. 24*
*Whitfield, pp. 188-189*

Rogers, Thomas
New Brunswick, 1783-84
Enslaved at least one female, Unus/Eanus Deaton.

Unus held a General Birch Certificate (GBC) of Freedom but Rogers re-enslaved her anyway. Unus also ran away with Peter Cox, Charity and her son Edward Morris.
*See Hubbard, Mat.*

In 1784, Rogers posted a runaway advertisement in the *Saint John Gazette*, seeking the return of six slaves/servants: Peter Cox, Edward & Charity Morris and their child, and Andrew and Eanus Bush. In his notice, Rogers also sought punishment for a "Mr. Dibble," who aided their escape. This likely refers to Fyler Dibblee, a prominent member of the Kingston Dibblee family.

Cox then moved to Milkish, where a large number of black refugees likely already lived. In 1785, he filed a petition on behalf of himself and twenty-two other black refugees. This petition was granted.

*(The) Milkish Settlement -*
*kingstonnb.ca/more/the-milkish-settlement*

Ryan, John
Saint John, 1799
Enslaved at least one person, name unknown (age 20).
*Whitfield, p. 200*
*The Royal Gazette, June 11th, 1799*

Ryan, John
(not certain if this is the same one as above)
New Brunswick, 1799
Enslaved at least two people, names unknown (19) and a child.
For Sale Advertisement was placed for the sale of these two people in the *Saint John Gazette*, April 12, 1799.
*Whitfield, p. 228*

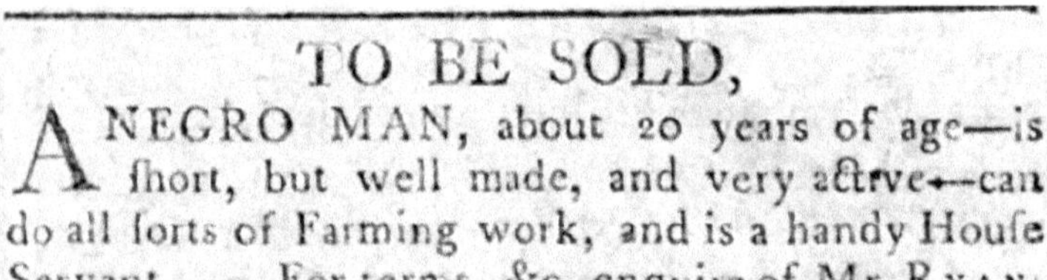

> ## TO BE SOLD,
> A NEGRO MAN, about 20 years of age—is short, but well made, and very active—can do all forts of Farming work, and is a handy Houfe Servant.—— For terms, &c. enquire of Mr. RYAN, Saint John, 11th June, 1799.

*Figure 70: A man to be sold*
...by Mr. Ryan.

Ryan, John
(not certain if this is the same one as above)
Saint John, dates unknown
Enslaved at least one person, Dinah (26). Bought her from James Taylor.

A Runaway Ad was placed for Dinah in the *Royal Gazette*, December 24, 1806

> CAUTION
> THE Subscriber hereby cautions all persons against attempting in future to seduce from his Service his Female Negro Slave DINAH, (for whom he has a good legal title)—as he is determined to punish by all legal ways and means, every offender of that description.—And that no one may plead ignorance of the person of the Slave in excuse, her informs all concerned that she is about 26 years of age—4 feet 9 inches high—has a small scar upon her forehead—and lately belonged to Mr. JAMES TAYLOR, of Maugerville.
> JOHN RYAN
> Saint John, 19th Nov. 1806
>
> *Chute, p. 51*

Ryerson, Peter
New Brunswick, 1788
Enslaved at least one person, Cesar Broadstreet
*Whitfield p. 30*

# S.

Scovill, James (Reverend)
Kings County
Enslaved Sampson (12); other people, names unknown
Scovill promised his slaves their freedom when they turned 26.
*Will of James Scovill (PANB)*
*Whitfield p. 167*

Seaman, Benjamin
Saint John County, 1785
Enslaved at least two males, Tom and Will.
*Will of Benjamin Seaman, 1785 (PANB)*
*Whitfield, p. 232*

Simmonds, James
River St. John, 1767
Enslaved one known person, West, whom he described as a 'rascal negro'.
*Smith, p. 11*
*Whitfield, p. 232*

Simpson, John
Maugerville, 1791
Enslaved one known person, John, who was described as a 'servant child'.
*Whitfield, p. 106*

Stewart, Charles
New Brunswick, 1786
Enslaved at least two people, man and woman, names unknown.
Stewart was selling his estate to include his "Negro Man and woman, slaves".
*Advertisement in the Royal Gazette, March 7, 1786*
*Whitfield, p. 226*

# T.

Taylor, James
Maugerville, 1805
Enslaved one woman, Dinah.
A Runaway Advertisement was published in *The Royal Gazette*, December 24, 1806, which describes Dinah as 'lately belonged to Mr. James Taylor".
*Chute, pp. 32, 51*

# V.

Van Dyne, Donn or Dow
Saint John (possibly), 1783
Enslaved at least one male, Jude (age 14).
*Book of Negroes*
*Whitfield, p. 108*

# W.

Wanton, William
Saint John County, 1812
Enslaved one male, Buck, age unknown.
*Whitfield, p. 31*

Ward, B (or J)
New Brunswick, 1783
Enslaved one child, Jeff (12)
*Book of Negroes*

Williams, Reuben
Gagetown, 1799
Enslaved one or two people, Dick and/or Gill.
They ran away together from their owners, Williams and James Peters.
*See Peters, James*
*Chute, p. 50*

**Brenda J. Thompson**

# Enslavers of Prince Edward Island

## Formerly known as Île St-Jean
## Also known as Epekwitk

## A.

Anderson, Peter
PEI, 1780s
Enslaved two people, names unknown.
*Whitfield, p. 209*

## B.

Beers, Joseph
PEI, 1780s
Enslaved two people, names unknown.
*Whitfield, p. 209*

Berry, Walter
PEI, dates unknown
Enslaved an unknown number of people, all names unknown.
*Whitfield and Cahill, p. 32*

*Bovyer, John*
Brudinell (sic) Station, dates unknown
Enslaved "a few", all names unknown.
*Whitfield and Cahill, p. 32*
*Whitfield, pp. 38-39*

> "The paternal great-grandfather, Rev. Stephen Bovyer,
> accompanied his son from Rhode Island to Prince Edward
> Island, being an aged man at the time. His son was
> supposed to have been a slave holder, as he brought two
> slaves with him, one of which was hanged at Charlottetown,
> after his emancipation for stealing a pint of rum."
> *data2.collectionscanada.gc.ca/080027/*
> *amicus-4651885_06.pdf, p. 340*

Burns, (Captain)
PEI, 1785
Enslaved one known person, Jupiter Wise, age unknown.
*Whitfield, p. 235*

# C.

Callbeck (Captain)
PEI
Enslaved one known person, Guy, who ran away in the Jupiter Wise
Conspiracy.
*King vs. Jupiter Wise*
*Whitfield, p. 76*

Clark, John
PEI, 1783
Enslaved an unknown number of people, names unknown.
*Whitfield and Cahill, p. 32*

Compton, (Colonel)
PEI, 1780s
Enslaved two people, both names unknown.
*Whitfield, p. 210*

Creed, William
PEI, dates unknown
Enslaved one known person, Suckles Dimbo.

> "It is believed that Suckles was kidnapped in Africa and
> brought to PEI. He eventually got his freedom and bought
> land for himself and his wife in Prince Edward Island."
> *Whitfield and Cahill, pp. 35-6*

## F.

Fanning, Edward (Lieutenant Governor)
PEI,1780s
Enslaved two people, David Sheppard and another, name
unknown.
*Whitfield and Cahill, p. 11*

## H.

Haszhard, Thomas
Charlottetown, 1802
Enslaved two people, Catherine (age 5) and Simon (3).
Catherine and Simon were considered Mulattos and were sold to
one of Haszhard's family members.
*Whitfield, p. 37*
*Whitfield and Cahill, p. 36*

> "Later that year, in Nov 1802, another private sale was re-
> corded that indicates the market value of a young mixed
> race slave. The conveyance was from 'Thomas Hassard Esq.

of Charlotte Town' to his son, 'William Hassard of lot #49' in repsect (sic) of 'a certain Mollatta Boy of three years of age called Simon with all his wearing aparrel(sic)'. 'Old Virginia' Tom Haszard had been a large landholder at Boston Neck, Rhode Island, who fought for the British during the American Revolution and who's (sic) property was confiscated by the Americans. He settled on the Island of St. John in 1785, and made two conveyances of Slaves before his death in 1804.

William Haszard bargained to pay his father 20 pounds Halifax currency for Simon, who may have been born to a female slave of the elder Haszard. A girl who was given to William's daughters Harriett and Louisa at the same time may have been Simon's sister: she is 'one Molatta Girl about five years of age, named Catherine,' the title to whom was warranted 'against any Claim or Demand Whatsoever'."

*Hornby, np.*

Haszhard, William
Charlottetown, 1802
Enslaved two children, Catherine (age 5) and Simon (3), whom he purchased from his father.
*Whitfield, p. 37*

Haszhard, Harriett and Louisa (sisters)
Charlottetown, 1802-1804
Enslaved one child, Catherine, who was given to them by their father, William.
*Hornby, np*

Hayden, Samuel
PEI, 1780s
Enslaved two people, both names unknown.
*Whitfield, p. 210*

Higgins, David
PEI, 1780s
Enslaved two people, both names unknown.
*Whitfield, p. 210*
*Whitfield and Cahill, p. 32*

Hurd, (Mr.)
PEI, 1780s
Enslaved two people, both names unknown.
*Whitfield, p. 210*
*Whitfield and Cahill, p. 32*


# O.

Ormsby, (Family)
PEI, 1828
Enslaved four people, Charles (age 20), Mary Jane (13), Fanny (11) and Edward (8).
This was very late in the history of enslavement in the Maritimes.
*Whitfield, p. 40-41, quoting the Montserrat Slave Register.*


# P.

Patterson, Walter (Governor)
Charlottetown, 1770-1785
Enslaved four people, Ben, Peg, Torriano and Susannha. Susannha was allegedly the mistress of Governor Patterson.

All except for Peg were involved in the Jupiter Wise conspiracy. Peg was not included as the others did not trust her.
*Whitfield, p. 20*

> The Jupiter Wise Conspiracy
> "...thanks to Jupiter Wise's theft of rum to supply a party in the summer of 1785, and a larger theft later that year, likewise to supply the necessities for a party, we learn that

it was not uncommon for African-Islanders together to have a good time and to discuss, among other things, plans to escape their unhappy situation. (Wise would eventually be brought to ground on both counts of theft, followed by assault. Although not charged for the former, he was sentenced to hang for the latter, a sentence later commuted to transportation from the Island to the West Indies, thanks to benefit of the clergy."

*Stewart, np*

"Jupiter Wise appeared in court on 22 February 1786 and three indictments were found against him, the burglary...and two assaults. He was acquitted of the burglary but found guilty of one of the assaults, which involved the use of a cutlass and was therefore a felony. At sentencing Wise escaped hanging by pleading benefit of clergy, and was sentenced to be 'transported for seven years to some one of His Majesty's Islands in the West Indies'. Wise and another prisoner awaiting transportation escaped from prison but were recaptured in Nova Scotia. Their fate is not known. "

*Holman, p. 101*

# R.

Robinson, Joseph (Colonel)
PEI, dates unknown
Enslaved six people, Ameila and Peter (married), their sons Edward and Jack, and William Byers and Sancho Campbell.

Sancho was hanged for stealing bread.
Peter Byers (aka Black Peter) was hanged 12 days after Sancho for stealing food from a local shop.
*Vol. 5 Canadian Biographical Dictionary*
biographi.ca/en/bio/byers_peter_5E.html
*See next page.*

"The saga begins in October 1814, when Sancho Byers, son of John 'Black Jack' and Amelia, was brought up and convicted on charges of having burgled the house of Matilda Brecken, the daughter of his former owner, helping himself to a single loaf of bread and about a shilling's worth of butter. That's it. Despite legal representation, Sancho was found guilty and sentenced to hang."

*Stewart, np*

# S.

Schurman/Schurmann, William
Bedeque, 1780s-1819
Enslaved "a few", including Black Bill and Susannah.
Susannah was mentioned in Schurman's Will: "She shall be provided for in the family...as long as she lives..."
*Whitfield, pp. 26, 178*

Smith, Alexander
PEI, 1780s
Enslaved two people, both names unknown.
*Whitfield, p. 211*

Strickland, John
PEI, 1780s
Enslaved two people, both names unknown.
*Whitfield, p. 211*

Stewart, Peter (Chief Justice)
PEI, dates unknown
Enslaved one known person, Peter, who was part of the Jupiter Wise Conspiracy.
*Whitfield, p. 142*

## T.

Throckmorton, John
PEI, 1780s
Enslaved two people, both names unknown.
*Whitfield, p. 211*

# Bibliography

Cahill, Barry and Harvey Amani Whitfield, "Slave Life and Slave Law in Colonial Prince Edward Island 1769-1825", in *Acadiensis* Vol. 38 No. 2 Summer/Autumn 2009.

*Canadian Biography, Dictionary of*  http://www.biographi.ca/en/

Chute, Sarah Elizabeth, *Bound to Slavery; Economic and Biographical Connections to Atlantic Slavery between the Maritimes and the West Indies after 1783,* graduate thesis, University of Vermont, 2021.

_____, *Runaway Slave Advertisements from Loyalist Newspapers of the Maritime Colonies*, Western Washington University, Fall 2018.

Clarke, George Elliott (editor), *Fire on the Water: An Anthology of Black Nova Scotia Writing, Volume Two,* Halifax: Pottersfield Press, 1992.

Clarkson, John, *Mission to America*, blackloyalist.com/cdc/documents/diaries/mission.htm

Cottreau-Robins, Catherine (Dr.), *Searching for the Enslaved in Nova Scotia's Loyalist Landscape*,

PhD. Dissertation, University of New Brunswick, May 2014.

Cousins, Leone B., *Diary of Captain John Clements, Nova Scotia*, Falcon Press, 1982.

Davidson, Stephen, "Loyalist Trails" uelac.ca/loyalist-trails/loyalist-trails-2008-41/

_____, "Carleton's Book of Negroes: A Ledger's Legacy (Part 2)", in Loyalist Trails 2016-35 uelac.ca/loyalist-trails/loyalist-trails-2016-35/#CarletonBook.

Dexter, Janetta, *Pioneers of the Mountain*, unpublished history of the communities of the North Mountain outside Bridgetown,

Halifax: Nova Scotia Archives MG4 Vol. 293, Binder 1.

Donovan, Kenneth, A Nominal list of Slaves and Their Owners in Ile Royale 1713-1760, in *Acadiensis* 25 (1),3, April 23, 2009, originally published 1995-10-10.

_____,"Female Slaves as Sexual Victims in Île Royale". in *Acadiensis* XLlll no. 1 (Winter/Spring 2014).

_____, "Slavery and Freedom in Atlantic Canada's African Diaspora: Introduction", journals.lib.unb.ca/index.php/acadiensis/article/view/22039/25571

_____, "Slaves and Their Owners in Île Royale 1713-1760", in Acadiensis XXV, n. 1 (Autumn 1995).

Eaton, Arthur, *The History of King's County, Nova Scotia*, Salem Press, 1910.

Frost, Karolyn Smardz and David W. States, *King's Scholarly Inquiry into its connections with slavery* (pdf), June 23, 2020.

*Granville Township Book*, NS Archives NSA MG 4 Vol 34.

Hamilton, Sylvia, "Potato Lady", in *Fire on the Water: An Anthology of Black Nova Scotia Writing* Volume Two, edited by George Elliott Clarke, Halifax: Pottersfield Press, 1992.

Harris, Frederick Wheeler, "The Negro Population of the County of Annapolis." Paper read at annual meeting of the Historical Association of Annapolis Royal, NS, 11 November 1920.

Hodges, Graham Russell, *Black Loyalist Directory: African Americans in Exile After the American Revolution*, Scholarly Titles, 1995.

Holman, HT, "View of Slaves and Servants on Prince Edward Island: The Case of Jupiter Wise", in *Acadiensis*, Vol. 12 No. 1, Autumn 1982.

Hornby, Jim, *Black Islanders*, Institute of Island Studies, 1991. islandregister.com/haszard1.html

Kimber, Stephen, *Loyalists and Layabouts; The Rapid Rise and Faster Fall of Shelburne, Nova Scotia 1783-1792*, Toronto: Anchor Canada, 2009.

Lohrenz, Otto, "Impassioned Virginia Loyalist and New Brunswick Pioneer: The Reverend John Agnew", in *Anglican and Episcopal*

*History*, vol. 76, no. 1, 2007, pp. 29–60. jstor.org/stable/42613039.

McConnell, Brian LLB, UE, *From Slave Owner's Son to the African Baptist Church* uelac.org/PDF/Land-Transfers-From-Slave-Owning-Loyalists-Son-to-the-African-Baptist-Church-by-Brian-McConnell.pdf

Mosher, Edith, *North Along the Shore*, Windsor: Lancelot Press, 1976.

_____, *Old Time Travel in Nova Scotia*, Windsor: Lancelot Press, 1984.

_____, *The Sea and the Supernatural*, Windsor: Lancelot Press 1985.

O'Brien, G. Patrick, "'Unknown and Unlamented' Loyalist Women in Nova Scotia from Exile to Reparation, 1775-1800", PhD dissertation, U. South Carolina, 2019.

Perkins, Charlotte, *The Romance of Old Annapolis Royal*, University of Michigan, 1934.

Perkins, Simeon(Colonel), *The Diary of Simeon Perkins Liverpool 1766-1780 vol. 1*

Robart-Johnson, Sharon, *Africa's Children; a History of Blacks in Yarmouth, Nova Scotia*, Toronto: Dundurn Press, 2009.

_____, *Jude and Diana*, Halifax: Fernwood Press, 2021.

Sherwood, Ronald H., *Pictou Pioneers*, Windsor: Lancelot Press, 1973.

Smith, Thomas Watson, *The Slave in Canada*, Collection of the Nova Scotia Historical Society, Vol. 10, Halifax: Nova Scotia Historical Society, 1899.

States, David W., "Presence and Perseverance; Blacks in Hants County, Nova Scotia 1871-1914", graduate thesis, St. Mary's University, 2002.

States, David W. And Karolyn Smardz Frost, *King's Scholarly Inquiry into its connections with slavery* (pdf), June 23, 2020.

States, Verna, *Growing Up Black*, Hansport: Hantsport and Area Historical Society mcdadeheritagecentre.ca/2021/08/01/growing-up-black-verna-irene-states/

Stewart, Isaac L., "A Harsh Sentence: African-Islanders, Slavery and Criminal Justice", peihistoryguy.com/2016/02/19/a-harsh-sentence-african-islanders-slavery-and-criminal-justice/

Thomas, Verna, *Invisible Shadows: A Black Woman's Life in Nova Scotia*, Halifax: Nimbus, 2001.

UNB Libraries, *Black Loyalists in New Brunswick*, atlanticportal.hil.unb.ca/acva/blackloyalists/en/

Unknown Author, *The Milkish Settlement*, kingstonnb.ca/more/the-milkish-settlement

Whitfield, Harvey Amani, *Biographical Dictionary of Enslaved People in the Maritimes*, Toronto: University of Toronto Press, 2022

_____, "The Struggle Over Slavery in the Maritime Colonies", in *Acadiensis* 2012 Vol. XLI No. 2 Summer/Autumn

Whitfield, Harvey Amani and Barry Cahill, "Slave Life and Slave Law in Colonial Prince Edward Island 1769-1825", in *Acadiensis* Vo. 38 No. 2 Summer/Autumn 2009.

Wilson, Isaiah W., *Geography and History of the County of Digby, Nova Scotia*, Holloway Brothers Publications, 1900.

Wright, Esther Clark, *The Loyalists of New Brunswick*, self-published at Fredericton, New Brunswick, 1955.

## Collections

Acadia University Archives - The Esther Wright Collection
   ~ Arthur Wentworth Hamilton Eaton Collection- 1900.011-EAT/5
   ~ Cornwallis Township Book - 1900.282-COR/1
   ~ Township of Parasboro book - 1900.031/1
   ~ Wiswall, John (Reverend), Journal of -1900.008-WIS

National Archives
   ~ Sir Guy Carleton Papers no. 10427, Kew PRO 30/55/100 (microfilm 10149)

Nova Scotia Archives
- ~ A.E. Cornwall Photo Collection
- ~ African Nova Scotians
- ~ Anglican Church of Digby, Records/Baptisms
- ~ Annapolis County Probate Records  RG 34-301 vol. P2; microfilm reel 12124
- ~ Annapolis County Supreme Court Records
- ~ Book of Negros
- ~ Chesley Papers
- ~ Clara Dennis Photo Collection
- ~ Colchester County Record of Deeds
- ~ Colchester County Register of Deeds
- ~ Cumberland County Probate Records
- ~ Documentary Art Collection
- ~ Eassons (the) and the Hoyts; Two Hundred Years of Family and Community Life in Nova Scotia (Collection)
- ~ Granville Township Records-(12323, Repository)
- ~ Halifax County Judgement Books- RG 39 J Halifax County volume 6 page 103
- ~ Hants County Court of General Sessions -
- ~ Kings' County Probate Records
- ~ James Cox
- ~ Muster Roll of Discharged and Disbanded Soldiers and Loyalists in the County of Annapolis June 1784 (microfilm 10163, pp. 28-53.)
- ~ Notman Studio Photo Collection
- ~ Nova Scotia House of Assembly Archives
- ~ Petition of John Taylor and Others- RG 5 series A volume 14 number 49 (microfilm 15591)
- ~ Pictou County Probate Records
- ~ Settlers at Country Harbour, Loyalist Musters 1776-1785 (MG23, D1., ser.1., vol. 24)
- ~ Shelburne County Court of General Sessions (RG 42 SH volume 1 file 4)
- ~ Shelburne County Probate Records
- ~ Shelburne Township Records

~ St. George's Anglican Church, Sydney, Records/Baptisms
~ St. Luke's Church of Annapolis Royal, Records/Baptism
~ Wentworth family Letters

## Newspapers

*Nova Scotia*
Acadian Recorder
Halifax Gazette
Nova Scotia Chronicle and Weekly Advertiser
Nova Scotia Gazette and Weekly Chronicle
Nova Scotia Packet and General Advertiser
Royal Gazette

*New Brunswick*
New Brunswick Courier
Royal Gazette
Saint John Gazette
The Royal Gazette and New Brunswick Advertiser

# Acknowledgements

No author writes a book alone, especially a book that focuses on history. This book has had a great deal of help from many people. I especially want to thank the following people for helping me with my research, giving me encouragement and support:

Dr. Harvey Amani Whitfield for all the research you have done which is getting the history of enslaved people out into mainstream reading. You've also helped with my research, as you will see by all the citations.

Dr. Karolyn Smardz-Frost for being encouraging of this manuscript, and for all your research into this subject.

Heather LeBlanc for Mapannapolis and helping me discover more research.

Micha Cromwell for reading over the manuscript.

Richard (Buck) Stevens for reading over the manuscript.

Jan Fancy Hull for proofreading and catching the smallest of my mistakes.

Linda Hulme Leahy for proofreading, editing and encouraging me to 'Stop asking permission'.

Tim Wilson, videographer extraordinaire, for his cover photo; and Rebekah Wetmore for the overall cover design

Andrew Wetmore for being an awesome editor.

My husband, Kent Folks, listened to me talk endlessly about the subject, gave suggestions, read over manuscripts and forgave me when he talked to me and I was so engrossed in the subject that I did not hear him...repeatedly.

My daughters, Gwynneth and Megan for being supportive and quiet when I've been writing.

And finally, to my Mom, who has been very supportive of me and my writing since I could hold a pencil.

# About the author

Brenda J. Thompson has been a local history buff and writer all her life. Plays, short stories, press releases, protest chants, non fiction, fiction...nothing escapes her pen. An anti-poverty activist by nature, writer by choice, Brenda has won awards for her writing.

In 2019, Brenda founded Moose House Publications to provide a platform for writing in and about rural Nova Scotia. As of December, 2023, Moose House has published more than 70 titles, many by first-time authors.

Brenda lives in Perotte, Nova Scotia, not too near to Annapolis Royal.

www.ingramcontent.com/pod-product-compliance
Lightning Source LLC
Chambersburg PA
CBHW061145120626
46546CB00005B/1938